CIRCULAR**knitting**REDEFINED™

EDITED BY KARA GOTT WARNER

HOUSE of
WHITE
BIRCHES

PUBLISHERS
SINCE 1947

CIRCULAR**knitting**REDEFINED™

EDITOR Kara Gott Warner
ART DIRECTOR Brad Snow
PUBLISHING SERVICES DIRECTOR Brenda Gallmeyer

MANAGING EDITOR Barb Sprunger
ASSISTANT ART DIRECTOR Nick Pierce
COPY SUPERVISOR Michelle Beck
COPY EDITOR Amanda Scheerer
TECHNICAL EDITORS Charlotte Quiggle, Kathy Wesley
TECHNICAL ARTIST Nicole Gage

GRAPHIC ARTS SUPERVISOR Ronda Bechinski
GRAPHIC ARTISTS Jessi Butler, Minette Collins Smith
PRODUCTION ASSISTANTS Marj Morgan, Judy Neuenschwander

PHOTOGRAPHY SUPERVISOR Tammy Christian
PHOTOGRAPHY Matt Owen
PHOTO STYLIST Tammy Steiner

Printed in China
First Printing: 2010
Library of Congress Control Number: 2009929822
Hardcover ISBN: 978-1-59217-272-6
Softcover ISBN: 978-1-59217-273-3

DRGbooks.com

1 2 3 4 5 6 7 8 9

WELCOME**knitters!**

Circular Knitting Redefined celebrates the art of circular knitting, and how, in some respects, we've redefined and created "new rules" about what circular knitting means.

As you move through each chapter, you'll encounter some inventive approaches to both in-the-round and flat back-and-forth knitting. Once you explore the wonderful world of circular knitting, you may look at using straight needles as an archaic, and almost static, way of working. I'm sure that this book will help open your horizons as a knitter, and you may realize that it's high time to put those straight needles to bed!

My "ah" moment came when I discovered the multi-dimensional world of knitting with circular needles. Not only did I find it easier to work with them no matter what the project, but I also found them to be more practical than using straight needles. This method is in many ways more dynamic than its traditional back-and-forth counterpart. Knitting circularly takes on an almost "sculptural" effect because you can shape various sections simultaneously and literally see your garment take shape while it's still on the needle!

This wouldn't truly be a circular knitting book without mentioning those trusty old double-point needles. We either love them or hate them, but without them, we wouldn't be able to make those I-cords that we adore, or get into those "tight" spaces where our circular needle would become too close for comfort!

The amazing craft of knitting is an unlimited and exciting journey of learning that can last a lifetime. It's my hope that when you pick up your needles, you experience something new and wondrous every time!

Kara Gott Warner

Kara Gott Warner, Editor

CONTENTS

BACK**and**FORTH**basics**

BUILD**a**FOUNDATION **from**THE**bottom**-UP

TAKE**it**FROM**the**TOP-**down**

STEPPING**it**UP**a**NOTCH:
knittingIN**new**DIRECTIONS

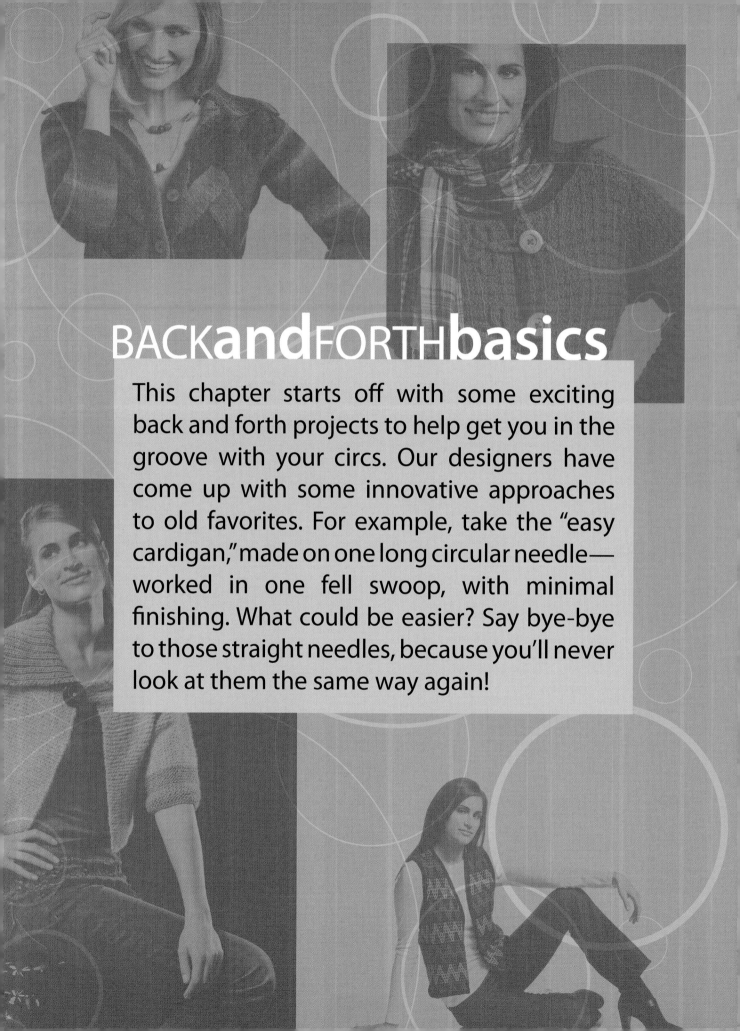

BACKandFORTHbasics

This chapter starts off with some exciting back and forth projects to help get you in the groove with your circs. Our designers have come up with some innovative approaches to old favorites. For example, take the "easy cardigan," made on one long circular needle—worked in one fell swoop, with minimal finishing. What could be easier? Say bye-bye to those straight needles, because you'll never look at them the same way again!

SPECIAL ways OF working

When building a house, we always start with the foundation. The same concept holds true for working in the round. This chapter is about exploring the circular needle and using it to construct back and forth projects. As you move through each chapter, you'll see how each builds upon the last, helping you to master each circular method along the way.

When first knitting back and forth on a circular needle, you may wonder how this is possible, considering a circular needle is traditionally intended for working a project in one continuous circle, such as a hat. The trick is to imagine that your circular needle is actually a set of straight needles. After working across a row, simply turn the needle around. The needle in your right hand now becomes the working needle.

Circs vs. Straight
The reasons are many for opting to use one circular needle over two straight needles. Here are a few to entice you:
- Easy Travel—They coil up in your knitting bag, which is a nice feature especially on a cramped plane. The person in the seat next to you will appreciate not being hit by the ends of your needles!
- You have no dangerous, pointy straight needles protruding out of your knitting bag.
- Your stitches can "stretch" out, giving you the ability to see your project as you go.
- When knitting a large number of stitches, the weight of the knitting is evenly distributed on a circular needle.
- Stitch patterns flow evenly around the garment—they are not interrupted by seams.

Deconstruct To Reconstruct
On the following pages, you'll see many familiar styles, but with a new spin: Instead of working in the traditional way by first working the back of the garment, then the front and then finally the sleeves, we suggest doing it all at once on a nice long circular needle. For example, you may work a cardigan starting from the bottom edge, working back and forth

from the left front, across the back, ending at the right front edge, all the while keeping your entire project neatly on one needle. Without having to deal with side seams, sewing is kept to a minimum. Working a garment in one piece may sound intimidating, but we promise you'll find it to be an easy and satisfying way to knit. The designs presented are both unique in construction and a breeze to make. You'll find that working on a circular needle brings fluidity to your back and forth projects, creating a natural rhythm to your knitting.

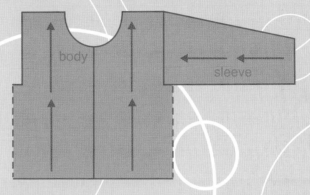

Visual Helpers
Each garment in the book is accompanied by a schematic, helping you to create "checkpoints" as you work through your project. If any adjustments are needed, you can fix these early in the process in order to save the tears later!

Illustrated above, the basic cardigan is worked flat, as one unit. The directional arrows indicate the direction to knit. In this scenario, your cast-on row starts at the bottom. The dotted lines indicate where the garment will be folded when worn. The center line indicates that this garment opens in front. Some important measurements to be aware of include: chest, body length, armhole depth, neck width and depth, shoulder width, sleeve length, sleeve cap height and width.

HOW TO When choosing a circular needle, it should be short enough so the stitches are not stretched when joined to work in the round. A circular needle can accommodate up to four times the original number of stitches. So if you want to use a different length, take note of the number of stitches to see if your chosen needle can accommodate them.

EASY**one-piece**CARDIGAN

DESIGN BY SARA LOUISE HARPER

Worked all in one piece, this little number knits up in a snap.

 EASY

SIZES
Child's 2 (4, 6, 8, 10) Instructions are given for smallest size, with larger sizes in parentheses. When only 1 number is given, it applies to all sizes.

FINISHED MEASUREMENTS
Chest: 26 (28, 30, 31, 32) inches (buttoned)
Length: 14 (15½, 16½, 18, 20) inches

MATERIALS
Berroco Comfort (worsted weight; 50% super fine nylon/50% super fine acrylic; 210 yds/100g per ball): 1 ball grape fizz #9708 (A), and 1 (2, 2, 3, 3) balls each berry mix #9805 (B) and raspberry sorbet #9728 (C)
Size 8 (5mm) 36-inch circular needle or size needed to obtain gauge
Stitch markers
5 (6, 6, 7, 8) buttons size, ⅝-inch diameter

GAUGE
18 sts and 34 rows = 4 inches/10cm in garter stitch.
To save time, take time to check gauge.

PATTERN NOTES
This sweater is worked in 1 piece from lower fronts to lower back. The 2 fronts are worked simultaneously; sleeves are cast on and worked sideways; the front neckline is shaped, then the 2 pieces are joined for back neck. After sleeves are complete, back is worked to lower edge.

When working color blocks, use intarsia method, using separate lengths of yarn for each colored section; bring new color up from under old color to lock them.

Tip: Work pocket for gauge swatch.

FRONTS
With A, cast on 32 (34, 36, 37, 38) sts for right front; with a 2nd ball of A, cast on 32 (34, 36, 37, 38) sts for left front.

Work in garter st for 1½ (1½, 2, 2, 2) inches, ending with a WS row. Cut A.

Using B for left front and C for right front, work even garter st until piece measures approx 5¾ (5¾, 6¾, 7, 7½) inches, ending with a WS row.

Buttonhole row (RS): *For girl's sweater,* work on right front as follows: K3, yo, k2tog; knit to end of row. *For boy's sweater,* work on left front as follows: Knit to last 5 sts, k2tog, yo, k3.

Rep Buttonhole row [every 12 rows] 3 (4, 4, 5, 6) times.

CAST ON FOR SLEEVES
At the same time, work even until fronts measure 8½ (9¾, 10½, 11½, 13¼) inches, ending with a WS row.
Next row (RS): Place a marker to separate

sleeve sts from front; cast on 5 (6, 5, 6, 6) sts at beg of row for left sleeve; knit across both pieces.

Next row (WS): Place a marker, cast on 5 (6, 5, 6, 6) sts at beg of row for right sleeve; knit across both pieces.

Continue to cast on 5 (6, 5, 6, 6) sts at sleeve edge of each front 7 (6, 8, 7, 8) more times—40 (42, 45, 48, 54) sts each sleeve.

SHAPE FRONT NECK

At the same time, after last buttonhole is made, work 9 rows on fronts, then shape front neck as follows:

Bind off 4 sts at each neck edge once, 3 sts once, 2 sts twice—21 (23, 25, 26, 27) sts each front.

Dec 1 st at each neck edge [every other row] 1 (3, 3, 3, 3) time(s)—20 (20, 22, 23, 24) sts each front.

Work even until fronts measure 14 (15½, 16½, 18, 20) inches, ending with a WS row;

this is "shoulder" line and center of sleeve; place a marker in the sleeve cuff to mark center of sleeve.

SHAPE BACK NECK

Cast on 5 (6, 6, 6, 6) sts at each neck edge twice—30 (32, 34, 35, 36) sts each side.

Next row (RS): Knit across all sts, twisting yarns at color join—60 (64, 68, 70, 72) back sts.

BIND OFF SLEEVES

Work even until sleeve cuff measures approx 7 (7½, 8, 8, 8½) inches or until "back" half of sleeve cuff measures same as "front" half of sleeve cuff, measuring from center sleeve marker.

Bind off 5 (6, 5, 6, 6) sts at beg of every row 8 (7, 9, 8, 9) times—no sleeve sts rem.

BACK

Work even until back measures same as fronts to lower band of A or approx 12½ (13, 14½, 16,

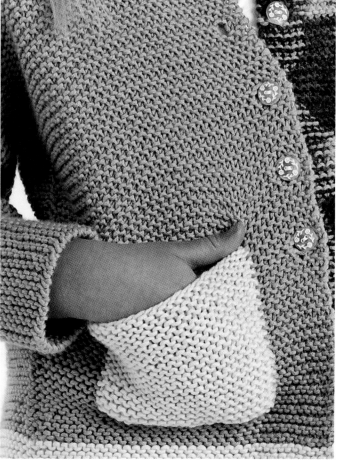

18) from shoulder line, ending with a WS row.
Cut B and C.

Join A; work even for 1½ (1½, 2, 2, 2) inches
or until back measures same as front.

Bind off all sts.

POCKET
With A, cast on 15 (18, 20, 20, 25) sts.

Work 3 (3½, 4, 4, 5) inches in garter st.

Bind off.

FINISHING
Weave in all ends; block to finished
measurements.

Sew sleeve and side seams.

NECKBAND
With A and beg at right front, pick up and knit
approx 60 (64, 68, 72, 76) sts around neckline.

Knit 1 row.

Work 1 Buttonhole row.

Knit 3 rows.

Bind off.

Sew buttons opposite buttonholes

Sew pocket to right front. ●

EASY ONE-PIECE CARDIGAN **SCHEMATIC**

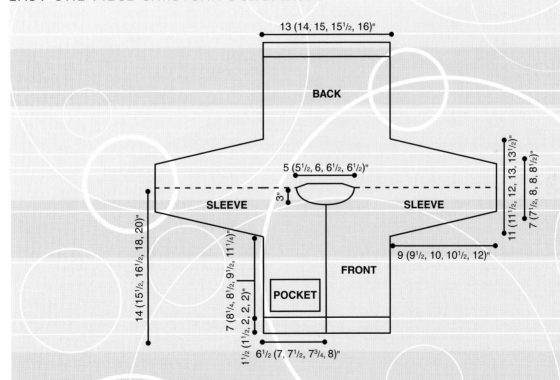

EVERYONE**loves**CHOCOLATE

DESIGN BY KYLEANN WILLIAMS

This lacy T-Top is easier than it looks, worked from the front edge over the shoulders to the back edge in one piece. What could be simpler?

◼◼◼◻ INTERMEDIATE

SIZES
Woman's small (medium, large, extra-large) Instructions are given for smallest size, with larger sizes in parentheses. When only 1 number is given, it applies to all sizes.

FINISHED MEASUREMENTS
Chest: 38½ (43, 47, 51) inches
Length: 23½ (25, 26, 26¾) inches

MATERIALS
Crystal Palace Panda Silk DK (DK weight; 52% bamboo/43% superwash merino wool/5% combed silk; 120 yds/50g per ball): 9 (10, 12, 14) balls cocoa blues #2001
Size 7 (4.5mm) 29-inch circular needle or size needed to obtain gauge
Stitch markers

3 LIGHT

GAUGE
24 sts and 32 rows = 4 inches/10cm in St st.
To save time, take time to check gauge.

SPECIAL ABBREVIATION
Place marker (pm): Place a marker on needle to separate sections.

PATTERN STITCH
Lace Panel (multiple of 6 sts + 9)
Row 1 (RS): P1, k1, [yo, ssk, k1, k2tog, yo, k1] 4 times, p1.
Row 2 and all WS rows: Purl.
Row 3: P1, k1, [yo, k1, SK2P, k1, yo, k1] 4 times, p1.
Row 5: P1, k1, [k2tog, yo, k1, yo, ssk, k1] 4 times, p1.
Row 7: P1, k2tog, [(k1, yo) twice, k1, SK2P]

3 times, [k1, yo] twice, k1, ssk, p1.
Row 8: Purl.
Rep Rows 1–8 for pat.

PATTERN NOTE
This boatneck top is worked back and forth in one piece, beginning at the front lower edge, going over the shoulders and back down to the back bottom edge. Sleeves are incorporated into the main body as it is knit.

FRONT
Cast on 109 (118, 132, 145) front sts; do not join.
Work in K1, P1 Rib for 2½ inches, ending with a WS row and inc 6 (11, 9, 8) sts on last row—115 (129, 141, 153) sts.
Set-up row (RS): K44 (51, 57, 63), pm, work Lace Panel, pm, knit to end.
Working side sts in St st and Lace Panel between markers, work even until piece measures approx 14 (15, 15½, 16) inches, ending with Row 8 of Lace Panel.

FRONT SLEEVES
Row 1 (RS): Cast on 42 (45, 48, 51) sleeve sts, pm, work established pat to end.
Row 2: Cast on 42 (45, 48, 51) sleeve sts, pm, purl to last 6 (6, 9, 9), pm, knit to end—199 (219, 237, 255) sts.
Maintaining first and last 6 (6, 9, 9) sts in garter st, rem sleeve sts in St st and front sts in established pat, work even until sleeve measures approx 6½ (7, 8, 8½) inches, ending with Row 8 of Lace Panel.

BOATNECK
Row 1 (RS): Knit to sleeve marker, work K1, P1 Rib to next sleeve marker, knit to end.
Row 2: K6 (6, 9, 9), purl to sleeve marker, work K1, P1 Rib to next sleeve marker, purl to last

BACK

6½ (7¼, 7½, 7¾)"

SLEEVE   SLEEVE

FRONT

23½ (25, 26, 26¾)"

19 (20, 21, 21½)"

14 (15, 15½, 16)"

9½ (10, 10½, 10¾)"

19¼ (21½, 23½, 25½)"

7 (7½, 8, 8½)"

LACE PANEL

6-st rep

STITCH KEY
- — P on RS, k on WS
- ☐ K on RS, p on WS
- o Yo
- ◥ Ssk
- ◢ K2tog
- ⋏ SK2P

6 (6, 9, 9) sts, knit to end.

Rep Rows 1 and 2 until sleeve measures 9½ (10, 10½, 10¾) inches, ending with Row 2.

Next row (RS): Knit to sleeve marker; work 38 (43, 48, 53) sts in established rib, bind off 39 (43, 45, 47) sts loosely in rib; work rib to next sleeve marker, knit to end.

Next row: K6 (6, 9, 9) sts, purl to sleeve marker, work 38 (43, 48, 53) sts in established rib, cast on 39 (43, 45, 47) sts, work rib to next sleeve marker, purl to last 6 (6, 9, 9) sts, knit to end.

Rep Rows 1 and 2 until back neck rib matches front neck rib, ending with Row 2.

BACK SLEEVES

Maintaining first and last 6 (6, 9, 9) sts in garter st, rem sleeve and side back sts in St st and working Lace Panel between center markers, work even until sleeve measures approx 6½ (7, 8, 8½) inches, ending with Row 8 of Lace Panel.

BACK

Bind off 42 (45, 48, 51) sts at beg of next 2 rows.

Work even in established pat until back measures same as front to bottom rib, ending with a WS row.

Next row (RS): Work in K1, P1 Rib and dec 6 (11, 9, 8) sts evenly across—109 (118, 132, 145) sts.

Continue in K1, P1 Rib for 2½ inches.

Bind off loosely in rib.

FINISHING

Weave in ends. Block to finished measurements.

Sew side and underarm seams. ●

EVERYONE LOVES CHOCOLATE **SCHEMATIC AND CHART**

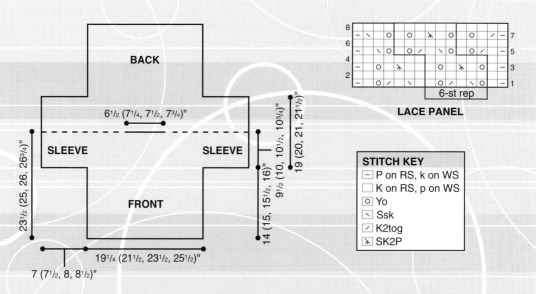

CAFÉ**aulait**CARDIGAN

DESIGN BY KARA GOTT WARNER

For a basic addition to your wardrobe, this easy garter-stitch cropped cardigan knits up in a flash.

 EASY

SIZES
Woman's small (medium, large, extra-large) Instructions are given for smallest size, with larger sizes in parentheses. When only 1 number is given, it applies to all sizes.

FINISHED MEASUREMENTS
Chest: 36 (40, 44, 48) inches
Length: 15 (16, 16½, 17) inches

MATERIALS
Plymouth Rainshadow (bulky weight; 98% baby alpaca/2% rayon; 88 yds/50g per ball): 7 (9, 9, 11) balls light fawn #2 (A)
Plymouth Mainland (worsted weight; 80% baby alpaca/20% silk; 71 yds/50g per ball): 1 (1, 1, 2) ball(s) fawn #3 (B)
Size 9 (5.5mm) 32-inch circular needle or size needed to obtain gauge
1 (2-inch) button

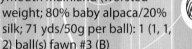

GAUGE
16 sts and 31 rows = 4 inches/10cm in garter st with A.
26 sts and 21 rows = 4 inches/10cm in K2, P2 Rib with B.
To save time, take time to check gauge.

SPECIAL ABBREVIATIONS
Make 1 (M1): Insert LH needle from front to back under the running thread between the last st worked and next st on RH needle; knit into the back of resulting loop.
Increase 1 (inc1): Knit in front and back of st.

PATTERN NOTE
Sweater is worked back and forth in one piece

from bottom to armholes, then divided into fronts and back which are worked separately; sleeves are worked back and forth.

BODY
With A, cast on 144 (160, 176, 192) sts; do not join.
Work even in garter st until piece measures 6½ (7, 7, 7) inches, ending with a RS row.

Divide for Armholes
Next row (WS): K32 (36, 40, 44) left front sts, bind off 8 sts for underarm, k64 (72, 80, 88) back sts [including st rem from bind-off], bind off 8 sts for underarm, k32 (36, 40, 44) right front sts [including st rem from bind-off].
Transfer left front and back sts to separate pieces of waste yarn, leaving right front sts on needle.

RIGHT FRONT
Work even until armhole measures 8½ (9, 9½, 10) inches, ending with a RS row.
Next row (WS): Loosely bind off 17 (20, 23, 26) shoulder sts, knit to end.
Transfer rem 16 (17, 18, 19) sts to waste yarn for front neck.

BACK

With RS facing, transfer back sts from waste yarn to needle and join A.

Work even until armholes measure 8½ (9, 9½, 10) inches, ending with a WS row.

Bind off 17 (20, 23, 26) shoulder sts at beg of next 2 rows—30 (32, 34, 36) sts.

Place rem sts onto waste yarn for back neck.

LEFT FRONT

With RS facing, transfer left front sts from waste yarn to needle and join A.

Work even until armhole measures 8½ (9, 9½, 10) inches, ending with a WS row.

Next row (RS): Loosely bind off 17 (20, 23, 26) shoulder sts, knit to end.

Transfer rem 16 (17, 18, 19) sts onto waste yarn for front neck.

SLEEVES

With B, cast on 52 (56, 60, 64) sts.

Working in garter st, work 3½ inches with B, then switch to A.

At the same time, shape sleeve as follows: Knit 6 (6, 6, 7) rows.

Inc row: K1, M1, knit to last st, M1, k1—54 (58, 62, 66) sts.

Rep Inc row [every 7 (7, 7, 8) rows] 7 (7, 3, 7) times, then [every 8 rows] 1 (1, 5, 0) time(s)—70 (74, 78, 80) sts.

Work even until sleeve measures 10 (10, 10½, 10½) inches.

Bind off.

FINISHING

Sew shoulder seams.

COLLAR

Transfer all neck sts from waste yarn to needle—62 (66, 70, 74) sts.

Row 1 (RS): Join B and knit across all sts.

Row 2: K1, inc1 in each st to last st, k1—122 (130, 138, 146) sts.

Row 3: K2, *p2, k2; rep from * across.

Work even in established rib until collar measures 6 inches.

Bind off loosely in rib.

BUTTON LOOP

With A, cast on 36 sts.

Work in garter st for 1 inch.

Bind off.

ASSEMBLY

Block pieces to finished measurements.

Sew sleeves to armholes, easing to fit. Sew sleeve seams.

Referring to photo on previous page, sew button loop to edge of right front.

Sew button to left front, centered under button loop.

Weave in ends. ●

CAFÉ AU LAIT CARDIGAN **SCHEMATICS**

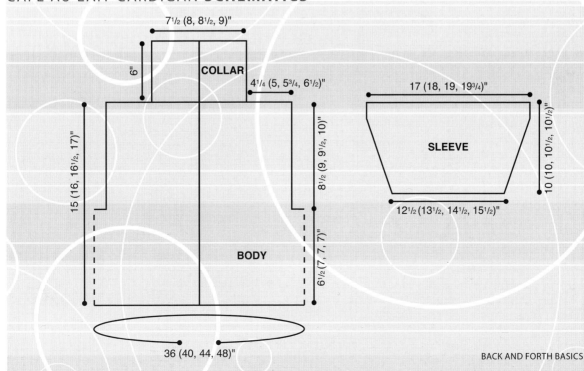

MYSTICAL**mosaic**VEST

DESIGN BY KATHARINE HUNT

Using a simple mosaic technique, this vest is knitted all in one piece to the armholes. Four bright colors are knit in zigzag bands over a contrasting base of black.

◼◼◼▢ INTERMEDIATE

SIZES
Woman's small (medium, large, extra-large) Instructions are given for smallest size, with larger sizes in parentheses. When only 1 number is given, it applies to all sizes.

FINISHED MEASUREMENTS
Chest: 37¼ (40, 44, 48) inches
Length to shoulders: 19¾ (20¾, 21¾, 22¾) inches

MATERIALS
SR Kertzer Super 10 Cotton (DK weight; 100% mercerized cotton; 249 yds/125g per skein): 2 skeins black #0001 (A); 1 skein each khaki #3609 (B), pear #3606 (C), ginger #3358 (D) and Persian #3995 (E).
Size 4 (3.5mm) 24-inch circular needle
Size 6 (4mm) 29-inch circular needle or size needed to obtain gauge
Stitch markers, 1 in CC for beg of rnd

(**3** LIGHT)

GAUGE
24 sts and 37 rows = 4 inches/10cm with larger needle in mosaic pat.
To save time, take time to check gauge.

SPECIAL ABBREVIATIONS
Wrap and Turn (W&T): Bring yarn to RS of work between needles, slip next st pwise to RH needle, bring yarn around this st to WS, slip st back to LH needle, turn work to begin working back in the other direction.
Place marker (pm): Place a marker on needle

to separate sections.
Decrease 2 (Dec 2): When working Seed st, dec 2 sts in pat over 5 sts by working 2 sts tog in pat, working 1 st in pat, working 2 sts tog in pat. This maintains the pat.

PATTERN STITCH
Seed Stitch (worked flat; odd number of sts)
Row 1: K1, *p1, k1; rep from * across.
Rep Row 1 for pat.

Seed Stitch (worked in the round; even number of sts)
Rnd 1: *K1, p1; rep from * around.
Pat rnd: Knit the purl sts and purl the knit sts.
Rep Pat rnd for pat.

Mosaic pat (multiple of 10 sts + 2)
See Chart.

Stripe sequence
When working Mosaic chart, *work 14 rows with A and B, 14 rows with A and C, 14 rows with A and D, 14 rows with A and E; rep from *.

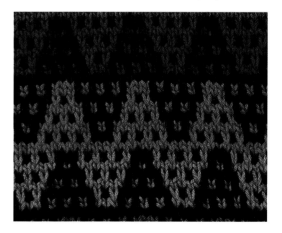

PATTERN NOTES

This vest is worked in one piece from the bottom up.

When working the mosaic pattern, always slip stitches purlwise with yarn held to the wrong side.

On the chart, the black squares represent A throughout; the white squares represent colors B, C, D and E, on successive color bands.

While shaping around the armholes and neckline, work the first and last st of each row in the working color for that row.

Bind off all stitches with smaller needle.

BODY

With smaller needle and A, cast on 212 (232, 252, 272) sts,

Work 5 rows in Seed st, beg and ending with a WS row.

Change to larger needle and work Mosaic pat and Stripe sequence following chart until piece measures 11½ (12, 12½, 13) inches, ending with a WS row.

Divide for back & fronts

Next row (RS): Work 38 (43, 45, 46) right front sts, bind off 24 (26, 30, 36) underarm sts, work 88 (94, 102, 108) back sts, bind off 24 (26, 30, 36) underarm sts, work 38 (43, 45, 46) left front sts; cut yarn.

Transfer front sts to separate pieces of waste yarn.

BACK

Row 1 (WS): Rejoin same color yarn as for previous row yarn and work across in pat.

Dec row (RS): K1, k2tog, work to last 3 sts, ssk, k1—86 (92, 100, 106) sts.

Maintaining pat, rep Dec row [every RS row] 4 (4, 5, 5) times—78 (84, 90, 96) sts.

Work even until armholes measure 8¼ (8¾, 9¼, 9¾) inches, ending with a WS row.

Shoulders

Row 1 (RS): Work to last 7 (7, 8, 9) sts, W&T.
Row 2: Work to last 7 (7, 8, 9) sts, W&T.
Row 3: Work to last 14 (14, 16, 18) sts, W&T.
Row 4: Work to last 14 (14, 16, 18) sts, W&T.
Row 5: Work to last 20 (22, 24, 26) sts, W&T.
Row 6: Work to last 20 (22, 24, 26) sts.

Cut yarn; turn work and slide sts to other end of needle.

With smaller needle and A, bind off all sts.

LEFT FRONT

Transfer left front sts back to needle.

Row 1 (WS): Rejoin same color yarn as for previous row yarn and work across in pat.

Dec row (RS): Join 2nd color; k1, k2tog, work to end of row—37 (41, 44, 45) sts.

Maintaining pat, rep Dec row [every RS row] 4 (4, 5, 5) times, ending with a WS row—33 (38, 39, 40) sts.

Neck

Dec row (RS): Work to last 3 sts, ssk, k1—32 (37, 38, 39) sts.

Rep Dec row [every 4 rows] 9 (12, 11, 10) times, then [every other row] 3 times—20 (22, 24, 26) sts.

Work even until armhole measures same as back, ending with a RS row.

Shoulders

Row 1 (WS): Work to last 7 (7, 8, 9) sts, W&T.
Row 2 (RS): Work to neck edge.
Row 3: Work to last 14 (14, 16, 18) sts, W&T.
Row 4: Work to neck edge.

With smaller needle and A, bind off all sts.

RIGHT FRONT

Transfer right front sts back to needle.

Row 1 (WS): Rejoin same color yarn as for previous row yarn and work across in pat.

Dec row (RS): Join 2nd color, work to last 3 sts, ssk, k1—37 (41, 44, 45) sts.

Maintaining pat, rep Dec row [every RS row] 4 (4, 5, 5) times, ending with a WS row—33 (38, 39, 40) sts.

Neck

Dec row (RS): K1, k2tog, work to end—32 (37, 38, 39) sts.

Rep Dec row [every 4 rows] 9 (12, 11, 10) times, then [every other row] 3 times—20 (22, 24, 26) sts.

Work even until armhole measures same as back, ending with a WS row.

Shoulders

Row 1 (RS): Work to last 7 (7, 8, 9) sts, W&T.
Row 2: Work to neck edge.
Row 3: Work to last 14 (14, 16, 18) sts, W&T.
Row 4: Work to neck edge.

With smaller needle and A, bind off all sts.

FINISHING

Block to finished measurements.
  Sew shoulder seams.

ARMHOLE BANDS

With RS facing, using smaller needle and A, beg at center underarm, pick up and knit 70 (73, 76, 79) sts to shoulder, pm, pick up and knit 70 (73, 76, 79) sts to center underarm—140 (146, 152, 158) sts; pm for beg of rnd and join.
  Work 3 rnds in Seed st.

Dec rnd: Work 10 sts in pat, *Dec 2 over next 5 sts, work 15 sts, Dec 2, work in pat to 2 sts before shoulder, Dec 2, work in pat to last 25 sts, Dec 2, work 5 sts, Dec 2, work to end of rnd—130 (136, 142, 148) sts.

Work 1 rnd in established pat.
With smaller needle, bind off in pat.

FRONT BANDS

With RS facing, using smaller circular needle and A, *pick up and knit approx 147 (155, 161, 169) sts evenly from bottom front of right front to center back neck.
  Work 5 rows Seed st.
  With smaller needle, bind off in pat.
  Rep on left front, working from center back neck to bottom front.
  Sew bands at center back neck. ●

MYSTICAL MOSAIC VEST **SCHEMATIC AND CHART**

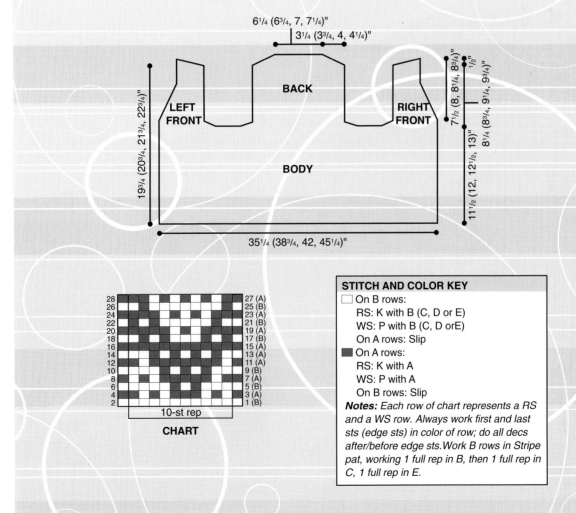

6¼ (6¾, 7, 7¼)"

3¼ (3¾, 4, 4¼)"

BACK

LEFT FRONT

RIGHT FRONT

BODY

19¾ (20¾, 21¾, 22¾)"

7½ (8, 8¼, 8¾)"

½"

8¼ (8¾, 9¼, 9¾)"

11½ (12, 12½, 13)"

35¼ (38¾, 42, 45¼)"

10-st rep

CHART

28 27 (A)
26 25 (B)
24 23 (A)
22 21 (B)
20 19 (A)
18 17 (B)
16 15 (A)
14 13 (A)
12 11 (A)
10 9 (B)
8 7 (A)
6 5 (B)
4 3 (A)
2 1 (B)

STITCH AND COLOR KEY

☐ On B rows:
  RS: K with B (C, D or E)
  WS: P with B (C, D orE)
  On A rows: Slip

■ On A rows:
  RS: K with A
  WS: P with A
  On B rows: Slip

Notes: *Each row of chart represents a RS and a WS row. Always work first and last sts (edge sts) in color of row; do all decs after/before edge sts.Work B rows in Stripe pat, working 1 full rep in B, then 1 full rep in C, 1 full rep in E.*

RESTAURANTEUR**shawl**

DESIGN BY LISA ELLIS

You'll want to cozy up in this shawl with "sleeves," sure to become a staple in your wardrobe.

INTERMEDIATE

SIZES
Woman's extra small (small, medium, large, extra-large, 2X-large) Instructions are given for smallest size, with larger sizes in parentheses. When only 1 number is given, it applies to all sizes.

FINISHED MEASUREMENTS
Width: 35–38 (37–40, 39–42, 41–44, 43–46, 45–48) inches, blocked
Length: 31 (32, 32½, 33¼, 33½, 34) inches

MATERIALS
Colinette Parisienne (DK weight; 70% kid mohair/30% polyamide; 243 yds/25g per hank): 4 (5, 5, 5, 6, 7) hanks Raphael #70
Blue Sky Alpaca Melange (sport weight; 100% baby alpaca; 110 yds/50g per hank): 10 (10, 11, 12, 13, 14) hanks huckleberry #805
Size 10 (6mm) 16- and 36-inch (or longer) circular needles or size needed to obtain gauge
Cable needle
Stitch marker

GAUGE
17 sts and 22 rows = 4 inches/10cm in Shadow Cable pat st with both yarns held tog.
16 sts and 20 rows = 4 inches/10cm in St st with both yarns held tog.
To save time, take time to check gauge.

SPECIAL ABBREVIATIONS
2 over 2 Left Cross (2/2 LC): Sl 2 to cn, hold to front, k2; k2 from cn.
2 over 2 Right Cross (2/2 RC): Sl 2 to cn, hold to back, k2; k2 from cn.

PATTERN STITCHES
Rib (multiple of 4 sts + 2)
Row 1 (RS): K2, *p2, k2; rep from * across.
Row 2: P2, *k2, p2; rep from * across.
  Rep Rows 1 and 2 for pat.
Shadow Cable (multiple of 8 sts + 10)
Row 1 (RS): Knit.
Row 2 and all WS rows: Purl.
Row 3: K1, 2/2 RC, *k4, 2/2 RC; rep from * to last 5 sts, k5.
Row 5: Knit.
Row 7: K5, *2/2 LC, k4; rep from * to last 5 sts, 2/2 LC, k1.
Row 8: Purl.
  Rep Rows 1–8 for pat.

PATTERN NOTES
Shawl is worked back and forth in one piece.
  Both yarns are held together throughout, including seaming.
  The shawl is stretched in blocking to achieve finished measurements.

SHAWL

With both strands of yarn held tog, cast on 154 (162, 170, 178, 186, 194) sts; do not join.

Work in Rib pat for 2 inches, ending with a WS row.

Change to Shadow Cable pat and work for 10 (10½, 10½, 11, 11, 11) inches.

Shape armholes

Bind off 8 sts at beg of next 2 rows—138 (146, 154, 162, 170, 178) sts.

Continue in established pat for 14 (14, 14½, 14½, 15, 15½) inches, ending with a WS row.

Using the backward-loop method, cast on 8 sts at beg of next 2 rows—154 (162, 170, 178, 186, 194) sts.

Continue in established pat for 10 (10½, 10½, 11, 11, 11) inches, ending with a WS row.

Work Rib pat for 2 inches, ending with a WS row.

Bind off all sts loosely in rib.

FINISHING

Sew side seams together from ribbed edge to armhole.

With 16-inch circular needle, pick up and knit approx 64 (64, 68, 68, 72, 76) sts around the armhole or as needed to prevent holes (st count must be a multiple of 4); place marker for beg of rnd. **Note:** *Rib edge worked in the round.*

Work K2, P2 Rib in the round for 2 inches. Bind off all sts loosely in rib.

Rep with other armhole.

Weave in all ends. Block, stretching to finished measurements given above, or as desired. ●

RESTAURANTEUR SHAWL **SCHEMATIC AND CHART**

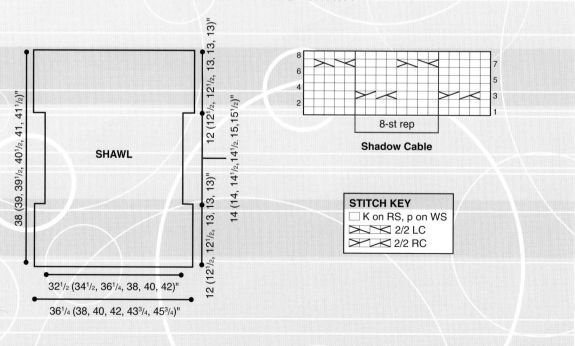

8-st rep

Shadow Cable

STITCH KEY
- ☐ K on RS, p on WS
- ⋈ 2/2 LC
- ⋈ 2/2 RC

SHAWL

38 (39, 39½, 40½, 41, 41½)"

12 (12½, 12½, 13, 13, 13)"

12 (12½, 12½, 13, 13, 13)"

12 (12½, 12½, 13, 13, 13)"

14 (14, 14½, 14½, 15, 15½)"

32½ (34½, 36¼, 38, 40, 42)"

36¼ (38, 40, 42, 43¾, 45¾)"

HUNKY**man**JACKET

DESIGN BY KATHARINE HUNT

A rugged stitch pattern and earthy, textured wool team up to make this zip-front hoodie a special gift for your man.

 **INTERMEDIATE**

SIZES
Man's medium (large, extra-large)
Instructions are given for smallest size, with larger sizes in parentheses. When only 1 number is given, it applies to all sizes.

FINISHED MEASUREMENTS
Chest (buttoned): 45½ (50, 54¼) inches
Length to shoulders: 25 (25½, 26) inches

MATERIALS
Tahki Donegal Tweed (worsted weight; 100% wool; 183 yds/ 100g per skein): 9 (10, 11) skeins dark red #863

4 MEDIUM

Size 4 (3.5mm) 24-inch circular needle or size needed to obtain gauge.
Size 7 (4.5mm) 30-inch circular needle
Stitch markers
Separating zipper to match yarn
Sewing needle
Thread to match yarn

GAUGE
18 sts and 28 rows = 4 inches/10cm in pat with larger needle.
18 sts and 25 rows = 4 inches/10cm in St st with larger needle.
To save time, take time to check gauge.

SPECIAL ABBREVIATIONS
Place marker (pm): Place marker on needle to separate sections.
Wrap and Turn (W&T): Bring yarn to RS of work between needles, slip next st pwise to RH needle, bring yarn around this st to WS, slip st back to LH needle, turn work to begin working back in the other direction.

Make 1 Right (M1R): Insert LH needle from back to front under the running thread between the last st worked and next st on LH needle. With RH needle, knit into the front of resulting loop.

Make 1 Left (M1L): Insert LH needle from front to back under the running thread between the last st worked and next st on LH needle; knit into the back of resulting loop.

Make 1 purlwise (M1P): Insert LH needle from front to back under the running thread between the last st worked and next st on RH needle; purl into the back of resulting loop.

SPECIAL TECHNIQUE
Hiding wraps: *On RS rows:* Pick up wrap from front to back and knit tog with wrapped st. *On WS rows:* Pick up wrap from the back, then purl it tog with wrapped st.

PATTERN STITCH
See chart.

PATTERN NOTES
The body of the sweater is worked in 1 piece from the bottom up, then separated for back and fronts. The shoulders are shaped using short rows. The sleeves are worked separately from the bottom up and sewn into the armholes. The hood is worked in 2 pieces which are sewn together, then sewn into the neck of the sweater.

Purchase zipper to fit after blocking sweater and knitting bands.

BODY
With smaller needle, cast on 199 (219, 239) sts; do not join.
Row 1 (RS): P1, *k1, p1; rep from * to end.

Continue in established rib until piece measures 2 inches, ending with a WS row and inc 1 st at end of last row—200 (220, 240) sts.

Change to larger needle; work even following chart until piece measures 15 (15, 15½) inches, ending with a WS row.

Divide for back & fronts
Row 1 (RS): Work 42 (45, 48) right front sts, bind off 12 (16, 20) underarm sts, work 92 (98, 104) back sts (including st rem from last bind-off), bind off 12 (16, 20) underarm sts, work 41 (45, 48) left front sts.

Cut yarn and put front sts on separate pieces of waste yarn.

BACK
Armholes
Row 1 (WS): Join yarn and work to end.
Dec row (RS): K1, ssk, work in pat to last 3 sts, k2tog, k1—90 (96, 102) sts.
Dec row (WS): P1, p2tog, work in pat to last 3 sts, ssp, p1—88 (94, 100) sts.

Work 5 (6, 7) more Dec rows—78 (82, 86) sts.

Work even until armholes measure 10 (10½, 10½) inches, ending with a WS row.

Shoulders
Row 1 (RS): Work to last 8 (8, 9) sts, W&T.
Row 2: Work to last 8 (8, 9) sts, W&T.
Row 3: Work to last 16 (16, 18) sts, W&T.
Row 4: Work to last 16 (16, 18) sts, W&T.
Row 5: Work to last 23 (25, 26) sts, W&T.
Row 6: Work to last 23 (25, 26) sts.

Cut yarn; turn work and slide sts to other end of needle.

Join yarn and using smaller needle, bind off all sts.

LEFT FRONT
Transfer left front sts back to needle with WS facing.

Armhole
Row 1 (WS): Join yarn and work to end.
Dec row (RS): K1, ssk, work in pat to end—41 (44, 47) sts.
Dec row (WS): Work in pat to last 3 sts, ssp, p1—40 (43, 46) sts.

Work 5 (6, 7) more Dec rows—35 (37, 39) sts.

Work even until armhole measures 7½ inches, ending with a RS row.

Neck
Row 1 (WS): Bind off 7 (7, 8) sts, work to end—28 (30, 31) sts.

Continuing in pat, dec 1 st at neck edge [every RS row] 5 times—23 (25, 26) sts.

Work even until armhole measures same as back, ending with a RS row.

Shoulder
Row 1 (WS): Work to last 8 (8, 9) sts, W&T.
Row 2 (RS): Work to neck edge.
Row 3: Work to last 16 (16, 18) sts, W&T.
Row 4: Work to neck edge.
Row 5: Purl to end.

Using smaller needle, bind off.

RIGHT FRONT
Transfer right front sts back to needle with WS facing.
Row 1 (WS): Join yarn and work to end.
Dec row (RS): Work in pat to last 3 sts, k2tog, k1—41 (44, 47) sts.
Dec row (WS): P1, p2tog, work in pat to end—40 (43, 46) sts.

Work 5 (6, 7) more Dec rows—35 (37, 39) sts.

Work even until armhole measures 7½ inches, ending with a WS row.

Neck
Row 1 (RS): Bind off 7 (7, 8) sts, work to end—28 (30, 31) sts.

Continuing in pat, dec 1 st at neck edge [every RS row] 5 times—23 (25, 26) sts.

Work even until armhole measures same as back, ending with a WS row.

Shoulder
Row 1 (RS): Work to last 8 (8, 9) sts, W&T.
Row 2: Work to neck edge.
Row 3: Work to last 16 (16, 18) sts, W&T.
Row 4: Work to neck edge.
Row 5: Knit to end.
Using smaller needle, bind off.

SLEEVES
With smaller needle, cast on 45 (47, 49) sts, do not join.
Row 1 (RS): K1, *p1, k1; rep from * to end.
Continue in established rib until piece measures 2 inches, ending with a WS row, and inc 1 st at end of last row—46 (48, 50) sts.
Change to larger needle and St st.
Work 4 rows.
Inc row (RS): K2, M1R, knit to last 2 sts, M1L, k2—48 (50, 52) sts.
Continue in St st and rep Inc row [every 4 rows] 19 (20, 19) times, then [every 6 rows] 3 times—92 (96, 96) sts.
Work even until sleeve measures 18½ (19, 19½) inches.
Mark each end, then work even for 1½ (1¾, 2) inches, ending with a WS row.
Dec row (RS): K2, ssk, work to last 3 sts, k2tog, k1—90 (94, 94) sts.
Rep Dec row [every RS row] 3 (4, 4) times—84 (86, 86) sts.
Bind off.

HOOD
Left Side
With larger needle, cast on 6 (6, 7) sts.
Knit 1 row.
Inc row (RS): K1, M1, knit to end—7 (7, 8) sts.
Inc row (WS): Purl to last st, M1P, p1—8 (8, 9) sts.
Continue in St st, inc 1 st at neck edge each row 9 more times—17 (17, 18) sts.
Next RS row: Using cable method, cast on 26 (26, 27) sts at beg of row for back neck—43 (43, 45) sts.
Work 3 rows even.
Rep Inc row on next, then [every 4 rows] 3 times—47 (47, 49) sts.
Work even until piece measures approx 12¾ inches, ending with a WS row.
Dec row (RS): K1, ssk, knit to end—46 (46, 48) sts.

Rep Dec row [every 4 rows] twice, then [every other row] 5 times, then every row once—38 (38, 40) sts.
Bind off all sts.

Right Side
With larger needle, cast on 6 (6, 7) sts.
Knit 1 row.
Inc row (RS): Knit to last st, M1, k1—7 (7, 8) sts.
Inc row (WS): P1, M1P, purl to end—8 (8, 9) sts.
Continue in St st, inc 1 st at neck edge each row 9 more times—17 (17, 18) sts.
Next RS row: Using cable method, cast on 26 (26, 27) sts at end of row for back neck—43 (43, 45) sts.
Work 3 rows even.
Rep Inc row on next, then [every 4 rows] 3 times—47 (47, 49) sts.
Work even until piece measures approx 12¾ inches, ending with a WS row.
Dec row (RS): Knit to last 3 sts, k2tog, k1—46 (46, 48) sts.
Rep Dec row [every 4 rows] twice, then [every other row] 5 times, then every row once—38 (38, 40) sts.
Bind off all sts.

FINISHING
Weave in loose ends; block pieces to finished measurements.
Sew shoulders invisibly. Sew back hood seam, from back neck to forehead.

Front Bands
With RS facing and smaller needle, beg at lower right front edge, pick up and knit 125 (125, 129) sts to neck.
Row 1 (WS): P1, *k1, p1; rep from * to end.
Work 5 more rows in established rib.
Bind off in rib.
Rep on left front, picking up from neck to lower edge.

Hood Band
With RS facing and smaller needle, beg at bottom front edge of right side, pick up and knit 95 (97, 101) sts along right side, 1 st in top seam, and 95 (97, 101) sts along left side; do not join—191 (195, 203) sts.
Complete as for front bands.

Beg at center back and working out to front neck edges, sew hood in place, easing around neck shaping, and taking care to align the bottoms of the hood bands with the tops of the front bands. Sew these band ends together.

Insert zipper so that front edges meet and conceal the teeth.

Set in sleeves, matching marked points to center underarm. Sew underarm seams. ●

HUNKY MAN JACKET SCHEMATICS AND CHART

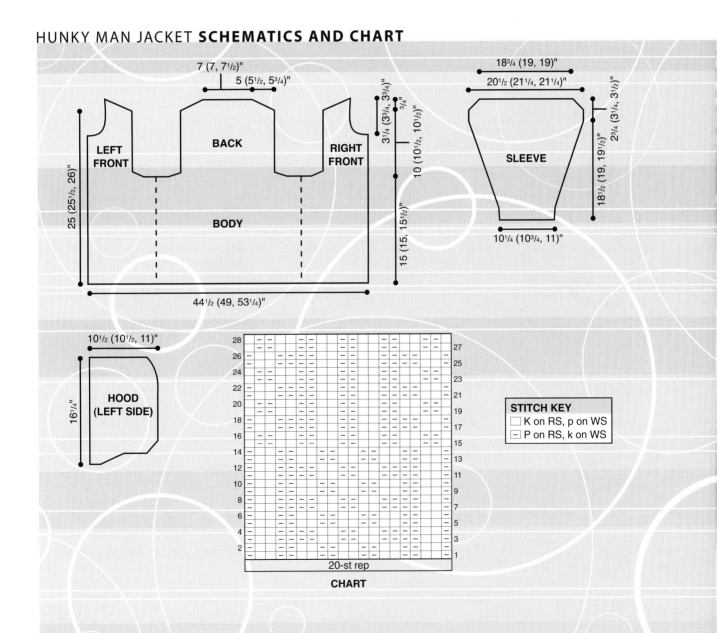

SWEETIE**pie**STRIPES

DESIGN BY LORRAINE EHRLINGER

This uniquely constructed cardigan will be a hit at the baby shower.

▬▬▬▭ INTERMEDIATE

SIZES
Infant's 0-3 (6, 12, 18, 24) months
Instructions are given for smallest size, with larger sizes in parentheses. When only 1 number is given, it applies to all sizes.

FINISHED MEASUREMENTS
Chest (unbuttoned): 23 (23½, 24, 25, 27) inches
Length: 8½ (9, 10, 10¾, 11¾) inches

MATERIALS
The Fibre Company Canopy Worsted (worsted weight; 50% baby alpaca/30% merino wool/ 20% bamboo; 100 yds/50g per skein): 2 (3, 3, 3, 3) skeins each blue quandons (MC) and ginger (CC)
Size 8 (5mm) 36-inch circular needle or size needed to obtain gauge
Size H/8 (5mm) crochet hook
Stitch markers in 2 colors
3 (1-inch) buttons
3 small flat buttons
Row counter (optional)

4 MEDIUM

GAUGE
19 sts and 38 rows = 4 inches/10cm in garter st. To save time, take time to check gauge.

SPECIAL ABBREVIATIONS
Place marker for increases (pm-i): Place a marker to indicate inc.
Place marker for decreases (pm-d): Place a marker to indicate dec.
Slip marker (sm): Slip marker as you come to it.

Make 1 (M1): Insert LH needle from front to back under the running thread between the last st worked and next st on RH needle; knit into the back of resulting loop.
Increase 1 (inc 1): Knit in front and back of the stitch.

PATTERN NOTES
This sweater is based on Debbie New's Maze sweater. The body is knit back and forth in mitered garter stitch; the sleeves are knit separately.

Decreases and increases will be worked on right side. Right side will have clear stripes.

The back numbers differ by one stitch because of marker placement; the two sides actually are the same on either side of the increases.

For ease in working, mark increases with 1 color marker and decreases with a different color marker.

Each outer button is backed with a flat button on WS to stabilize it.

The sweater is sized generously; if desired, place buttons further from edge when Baby is small, then move closer to edge as Baby grows.

BODY
With MC, cast on 222 (234, 246, 258, 280) sts.
Set-up row (WS): With MC, k32 (35, 38, 40, 44), pm-d, k1, pm-d, k55 (56, 57, 59, 64), pm-d, k1, pm-d, k22 (23, 25, 27, 29), pm-i, k1, pm-i, k21 (23, 25, 27, 29), pm-d, k1, pm-d, k55 (56, 57, 59, 64), pm-d, k1, pm-d, k32 (35, 38, 40, 44).
Row 2 (RS): With CC, knit to 2 sts before marker, k2tog, sm; k1; sm, k2tog, knit to 2 sts before marker, k2tog, sm; k1; sm, k2tog, knit to 1 st before marker, inc 1, sm; M1, k1, M1; sm, inc 1, knit to 2 sts before marker, k2tog, sm; k1; sm, k2tog, knit to 2 sts before marker, k2tog, sm; k1; sm, k2tog, knit to end—4 sts dec'd.

Row 3 and all WS rows: Knit with same color as previous row.

Row 4: With MC, knit to 2 sts before marker, k2tog, sm; k1; sm, k2tog, knit to 2 sts before marker, k2tog, sm; k1; sm, k2tog, knit to 1 st before marker, inc 1, sm; inc 1, knit to 1 st before marker, inc 1; sm, inc 1, knit to 2 sts before marker, k2tog, sm; k1; sm, k2tog, knit to 2 sts before marker, k2tog, sm; k1; sm, k2tog, knit to end—4 sts dec'd.

Continue working 2 decs at 4 corners and 4 incs at center back as on Row 4 and alternating colors every RS row.

At the same time, work buttonholes on Row 5 for girls/Row 6 for boys as follows: *K3, yo, k2tog, k5; rep from * twice more, then complete row as established.

Continue dec and inc as established through Row 9.

Neck Shaping

Row 10 (Neck Inc): Inc 1 in first and last sts. Continue dec and inc as established for 11 rows.

Row 22: Rep Neck Inc row.

Continue dec and inc as established for 3 rows.

Row 26: Rep Neck Inc row.

Rep Neck Inc row [every RS row] 3 (3, 3, 4, 4) times.

Cast on 2 (2, 4, 4, 5) sts at beg of next 2 rows.

Work even until piece measures approx 4¼ (4½, 4¾, 5, 5½) inches.

Bind off all sts loosely.

SLEEVES

With MC, cast on 29 (30, 30, 31, 31) sts.

Row 1 and all WS rows: Knit with same color as previous rows.

Rows 2 and 4 (RS): Knit, alternating MC and CC as for body.

Row 6 (Inc row): K1, inc 1, knit to last st, inc 1, k1—31 (32, 32, 33, 33) sts.

Maintain stripe pat and rep Inc row [every 6 rows] 7 (8, 9, 11, 12) times—45 (48, 50, 55, 57) sts.

Work even until piece measures 8 (9, 10, 11, 12½) inches.

Bind off loosely.

FINISHING

Weave in ends and block to finished measurements.

Sew center back slit. Sew shoulder seams. Sew sleeve into armhole opening. Sew underarm seam.

Sew buttons opposite buttonholes, sewing 2 buttons at once with flat button on inside of fabric and "outer" button on outside. ●

SWEETIE PIE STRIPES **SCHEMATICS**

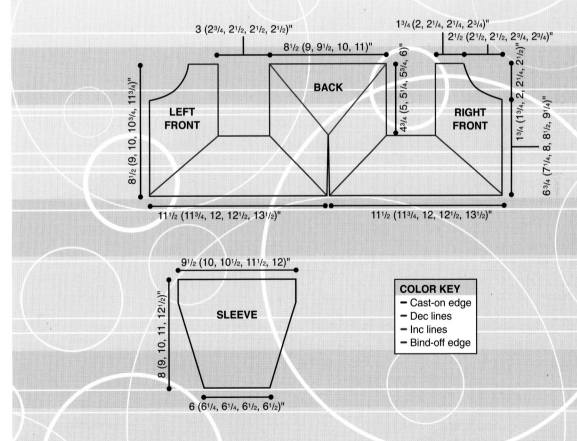

ALL**about**ENTRELAC

DESIGN BY ANDRA KNIGHT-BOWMAN

Try your hand at this alluring design, and discover the exciting art of entrelac.

■■■■ EXPERIENCED

SIZES
Woman's small (medium, large, extra-large, 2X-large) Instructions are given for smallest size, with larger sizes in parentheses. When only 1 number is given, it applies to all sizes.

FINISHED MEASUREMENTS
Chest: 38 (42, 46, 50, 54) inches
Length: 21½ (21½, 25½, 25½, 25½) inches

MATERIALS
Plymouth Boku (worsted weight; 95% wool/5% silk; 99 yds/50g per ball): 9 (11, 13, 14, 15) balls plums #11
Size 6 (4mm) double-point, 16- and 32-inch circular needles
Size 8 (5mm) double-point, 16- and 32-inch circular needles or size needles to obtain gauge
Stitch markers
6 (6, 7, 7, 7) 1-inch buttons

4 MEDIUM

GAUGE
16 sts and 20 rows = 4 inches/10cm in St st on larger needle.
To save time, take time to check gauge.

SPECIAL ABBREVIATION
Make 1 (M1): Insert LH needle from front to back under the running thread between the last st worked and next st on RH needle; knit into the back of resulting loop.

SPECIAL TECHNIQUE
3-Needle Bind-Off
With RS tog and needles parallel, using a 3rd needle, knit tog a st from the front needle with 1 from the back. *Knit tog a st from the front and back needles, and slip the first st over the 2nd to bind off. Rep from * across until indicated number of sts have been bound off.

PATTERN NOTES
Back and fronts are worked separately in entrelac from the bottom up; after shoulder seams are sewn, gussets are picked up from sides of body and worked out until piece is desired width, at which point side seams are joined using 3-Needle Bind-Off. The remaining sleeve stitches are worked in the round down to the cuff. Waist, front bands and collar are added at the end.

Each tier of the entrelac is written out as a step. Step 1 is the base triangles; Step 2 includes the right-edge triangle, a series of left-leaning rectangles and the left-edge triangle; Step 3 is a series of right-leaning rectangles. Steps 2 and 3 are repeated until and then the entrelac section is completed by working Step 4, the top triangles.

When working sleeves, change to double-point needles when stitches no longer fit comfortably on circular needle.

BACK
Step #1
Bottom edge triangles
With larger needle, cast on 40 sts, placing a marker every 10 sts.
Row 1 (WS): P2, turn.

Row 2: K2, turn.
Row 3: P3, turn.
Row 4: K3, turn.
Row 5: P4, turn.
Row 6: K4, turn.
Row 7: P5, turn.
Row 8: K5, turn.
Row 9: P6, turn.
Row 10: K6, turn.
Row 11: P7, turn.
Row 12: K7, turn.
Row 13: P8, turn.
Row 14: K8, turn.
Row 15: P9, turn.
Row 16: K9, turn,
Row 17: P10, do not turn, slip marker.

Rep from Row 1, leaving the 10 sts in each group on RH needle when completed, until all 40 sts have been worked. Turn work.

Step #2:
Right-edge triangle
Row 1 (RS): K2, turn.
Row 2: P2, turn.
Row 3: K1, M1, ssk.
Row 4: P3, turn.
Row 5: K1, M1, k1, ssk, turn.
Row 6: P4, turn.
Row 7: K1, M1, knit to 1 st before gap, ssk, turn.
Row 8: P5, turn.
Continue in this manner with 1 more st on RH needle until there are 10 sts.
Do not turn.

Left-leaning rectangle
With RS facing, pick up and knit 10 sts along side edge of base triangle, turn.
Row 1 (WS): P10, turn
Row 2 (RS): K9, ssk, turn.
Rep Rows 1 and 2 until all sts from right edge of adjacent base triangle have been worked into new rectangle.
Rep left-leaning rectangle twice more.

Left-edge triangle
With RS facing, pick up and knit up 10 sts along left edge of triangle, turn.
Row 1 (WS): P2 tog, p8, turn.
Row 2 (RS): K9, turn.
Row 3: P2tog, p7, turn.
Row 4: K8, turn.
Continue in this manner working 1 fewer st each row until 1 st rem. Do not turn.

Step #3
Right-leaning rectangle
With WS facing, pick up and purl 9 sts, turn—10 sts.
Row 1 (RS): K10, turn.
Row 2: P9, p2tog, turn.
Rep Rows 1 and 2 until all sts of previous rectangle have been worked in new rectangle; do not turn after finishing last row.
Rep right-leaning rectangle 3 more times across, picking up 10 sts to begin.
Rep [Steps 2 and 3] 3 (3, 4, 4, 4) times, then rep Step 1 once more.

Step #4
Top triangle
With WS facing, pick up and purl 10 sts along previous rectangle, turn—11 sts.
Row 1 (RS): K9, ssk, turn.
Row 2: P9, p2tog, turn.
Row 3: K8, ssk, turn.
Row 4: P8, p2tog, turn.
Row 5: K7, ssk, turn.
Row 6: P7, p2tog, turn.
Row 7: K6, ssk, turn.
Row 8: P6, p2tog, turn.
Row 9: K5, ssk, turn.
Row 10: P5, p2tog, turn.
Row 11: K4, ssk, turn.
Row 12: P4, p2tog, turn.
Row 13: K3, ssk, turn.
Row 14: P3, p2tog, turn.
Row 15: K2, ssk, turn.
Row 16: P2, p2tog, turn.
Row 17: K1, ssk, turn.
Row 18: P1, p2tog, turn.
Row 19: Ssk, turn.
Row 20: P2tog; do not turn.
Continue to make triangles across top; fasten off last st.

FRONT
Make 2
With larger needle, cast on 20 sts.
Work steps same as for back; fronts will have only 1 left-leaning and 2 right-leaning rectangle(s).

SIDE GUSSETS
Sew shoulders tog, leaving 7¾ (8, 8¼, 8½, 8¾, 9) inch opening for neck.
With RS facing and using larger 32-inch needle, beg at lower edge, pick up and knit 82 (82, 98,

98, 98) sts along 1 side to shoulder, then 82 (82, 98, 98, 98) sts along the side from shoulder down—164 (164, 196, 196, 196) sts.

Beg with a WS row, knit 3 rows.

Change to St st and work even for 2 (3, 4, 5, 6) inches, ending with a WS row.

With RS tog and needle points facing same direction, join side seam using 3-Needle Bind-Off, binding off first 52 (50, 65, 63, 61) sts—60 (64, 68, 72, 76) sts rem.

SLEEVES

Turn work so that RS is facing out; transfer sts to larger 16-inch needle.

Pick up and knit 1 st at the seam, knit rem sts, pick up and knit 1 more st at seam, place marker for beg of rnd and join—62 (66, 70, 74, 78) sts.

Knit 10 rnds.

Dec rnd: K1, ssk, knit to 3 sts before marker, k2tog, k1—60 (64, 68, 72, 76) sts.

Rep Dec rnd [every 6 rnds] 12 times—36 (40, 44, 48, 52) sts.

Work even until sleeve measures 16 (16½, 16½, 16, 16) inches or approx 1 inch short of desired length.

Change to smaller needles.

[Knit 1 rnd, purl 1 rnd] 6 times.

Bind off very loosely.

WAISTBAND

With RS facing and using smaller needle, beg at left front, pick up and knit 152 (168, 184, 200, 216) sts around lower edge; do not join.

Knit 12 rows.

Bind off very loosely.

BUTTONBAND

With RS facing and using smaller needle, beg at top, pick up and knit 82 (82, 97, 97, 97) sts along left front edge.

Knit 12 rows.

Bind off loosely.

BUTTONHOLE BAND

With RS facing and using smaller needle, beg at waistband, pick up and knit 82 (82, 97, 97, 97) sts along right front edge.

Knit 5 rows.

Buttonhole row: K3, [yo, k2tog, k13] 5 (5, 6, 6, 6) times, end yo, k2tog, k2.

Knit 5 rows.

Bind off loosely.

COLLAR

With WS facing and using smaller needle, beg at left front, pick up and knit 70 (72, 74, 78, 82) sts around neckline.

Knit 3 rows.

Next row: K1, M1, knit to last st, M1, k1—72 (74, 76, 80, 84) sts.

Next 3 rows: Knit.

Rep [last 4 rows] 7 times—86 (88, 90, 94, 98) sts.

Bind off loosely.

FINISHING

Weave in all ends. Block to finished measurements.

Sew buttons to buttonband opposite buttonholes. ●

ALL ABOUT ENTRELAC **SCHEMATIC**

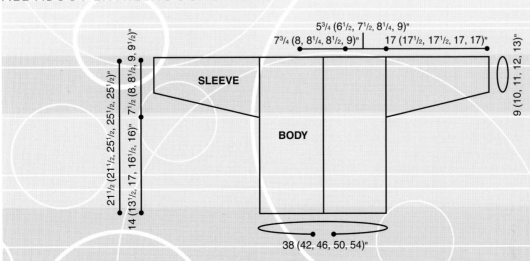

TRIBECA**belted**CARDIGAN

DESIGN BY AMY POLCYN

This warm and cozy cardigan is perfect for a stroll on a sunny autumn afternoon.

 INTERMEDIATE

SIZES
Woman's small (medium, large, extra-large, 2X-large) Instructions are given for smallest size, with larger sizes in parentheses. When only 1 number is given, it applies to all sizes.

FINISHED MEASUREMENTS
Chest: 36 (40, 44, 48, 52) inches
Length: 25¾ (27¾, 28½, 30, 31) inches

MATERIALS
Nashua Handknits Natural Focus Ecologie Wool (Aran/heavy worsted; 100% naturally dyed wool; 87 yds/50g per ball): 12 (13, 14, 16, 17) balls quebracho #NFW.0081
Size 9 (5mm) double-point (set of 5) and 32-inch circular needles or size needed to obtain gauge
Size I/9 (5.5mm) crochet hook
Stitch markers
1 (2-inch) belt buckle

4 MEDIUM

GAUGE
16 sts and 20 rows = 4 inches/10cm in St st.
To save time, take time to check gauge.

SPECIAL ABBREVIATIONS
Place marker (pm): Place a marker on needle to separate sections.
Make 1 Right (M1R): Insert LH needle from back to front under the running thread between the last st worked and next st on LH needle. With RH needle, knit into the front of resulting loop.
Make 1 Left (M1L): Insert LH needle from front to back under the running thread between the last st worked and next st on LH needle; knit into the back of resulting loop.

PATTERN NOTES
Cardigan is worked in one piece to the armholes. Sleeves are worked circularly to the armholes, then all pieces are united and worked to the neck. Shawl collar is worked using short rows. Belt is worked using double knitting.

INSTRUCTIONS
BODY
With circular needle, cast on 36 (40, 44, 48, 52) front sts, pm, cast on 70 (78, 86, 94, 102) back sts, pm, cast on 36 (40, 44, 48, 52) front sts, do not join—142 (158, 174, 190, 206) sts.
Row 1 (RS): K2, *p2, k2; rep from * to end.
Continue in established rib until piece measures 4 inches.
Change to St st and work even until piece measures 13 (13½, 14, 14½, 15) inches, ending with a WS row.

Beg neck shaping

Dec row (RS): K1, ssk, work to last 3 sts, k2tog, k1—140 (156, 172, 188, 204) sts.

Rep Dec row every 4 rows until piece measures 16 (16½, 17, 17½, 18) inches, ending with a WS row, then set body aside.

Note: *Neck shaping will continue after body and sleeves are joined.*

SLEEVES

With dpns, cast on 36 (36, 40, 40, 44) sts; pm and join, taking care not to twist sts.

Work 4 inches in K2, P2 Rib.

Knit 3 rnds.

Inc rnd: K1, M1R, knit to last st, M1L, k1—38 (38, 42, 42, 46) sts.

Rep last 4 rnds 9 (11, 11, 13, 13) times—56 (60, 64, 68, 72) sts.

Work even until sleeve measures 17 (17½, 18, 18½, 19) inches or desired length.

Place 4 sts each side of marker (8 total) on waste yarn; place rem 48 (52, 56, 62, 64) sts on spare circular needle for holder.

Set aside.

JOIN SLEEVES AND BODY

With RS of body facing, continuing neck shaping, if required, work to 4 sts before first marker; place next 8 sts on waste yarn, removing marker, pm; knit across sleeve sts, pm; knit across back to 4 sts before marker; place next 8 sts on waste yarn, removing

marker, pm; knit across sleeve sts, pm; work rem front sts.

RAGLAN YOKE

Continue neck shaping as established throughout, working neck decs a total of 13 (14, 15, 16, 17) times, then working even.

At the same time, work even in St st for 1 inch, ending with a WS row, then beg raglan shaping as follows:

Row 1 (RS): *Knit to 3 sts before marker, k2tog, k1, slip marker, k1, ssk; rep from * across.

Row 2: Purl.

Rep [Rows 1 and 2] 18 (20, 22, 24, 26) times—52 (58, 64, 70, 76) sts.

Bind off.

FINISHING

Graft underarms using Kitchener st.

SHAWL COLLAR & FRONT BANDS

With RS facing and circular needle, pick up and knit 238 (250, 262, 274, 286) sts along fronts and back neck.

Row 1 (WS): K2, *p2, k2; rep from * to end, placing markers at beg of neck shaping on each side.

Row 2 (RS): Work in established rib to 2 sts before farthest marker, turn.

Row 3: Sl 1 pwise, work in rib to 2 sts before marker, turn.

Row 4: Sl 1 pwise, work in rib to 2 sts before gap made by last short row, turn.

Rep Row 4 until collar measures 6 inches, ending with a WS row.

Next row (RS): Work in pat to end of row.

Working on all sts, continue in rib until front bands measure 1 inch.

Bind off in rib.

BELT

With dpns, cast on 16 sts.

Row 1: *Sl 1 pwise wyif, k1; rep from * across.

Rep Row 1 until belt measures 8 inches longer than waist, approx 34 (36, 38, 40, 42) inches.

Last row: K2tog across—8 sts.

Bind off.

Fold end of belt over center post of belt buckle and sew in place.

BELT LOOPS

Try on cardigan and mark waist at sides. Insert crochet hook into fabric at marked waist point and make a chain long enough to go around belt; pull last st to WS at same point and fasten off. Rep on other side.

Weave in ends. Block to finished measurements. ●

TRIBECA BELTED CARDIGAN **SCHEMATIC**

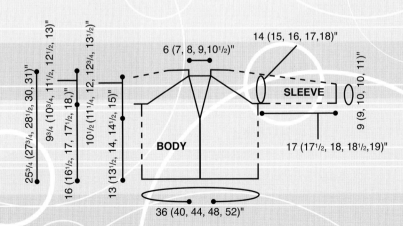

ENCHANTED**forest**

DESIGN BY SARA LOUISE HARPER

When you pull out your woolies, this coat will be the perfect accompaniment on a brisk winter outing.

INTERMEDIATE

SIZES
Woman's extra-small (small, medium, large, extra-large) Instructions are given for smallest size, with larger sizes in parentheses. When only 1 number is given, it applies to all sizes.

FINISHED MEASUREMENTS
Chest: 38 (42, 46, 50, 54) inches (buttoned)
Length: 25½ (26½, 27½, 28, 29) inches

MATERIALS
Brown Sheep Lamb's Pride
　Worsted (worsted weight; 85% wool/15% mohair; 190 yds/113g per skein): 12 (14, 16, 18, 20) skeins old sage #M69
Size 10 (6mm) 36-inch (or longer) circular needle or size needed to obtain gauge
Size 8 (5mm) needles for I-cord
Stitch holders
3 buttons (1⅝-inch diameter)

4 MEDIUM

GAUGE
16 sts and 24 rows = 4 inches/10cm in Welted Rib with yarn doubled.
To save time, take time to check gauge.

SPECIAL ABBREVIATIONS
Wrap and Turn (W&T): Bring yarn to RS of work between needles, slip next st pwise to RH needle, bring yarn around this st to WS, slip st back to LH needle, turn work to begin working back in the other direction.
M1R (Make 1 Right): Insert LH needle from back to front under the running thread between the last st worked and next st on LH needle. With RH needle, knit into the front of resulting loop.
M1L (Make 1 Left): Insert LH needle from front to back under the running thread between the last st worked and next st on LH needle; knit into the back of resulting loop.

PATTERN STITCH
Welted Rib (multiple of 3 sts + 1)
Row 1 (RS): K1, *p2, k1; rep from * across row.
Row 2: P1, *k2, p1; rep from * across row.
Row 3: Knit.
Row 4: Purl.
　Rep Rows 1–4 for pat.

SPECIAL TECHNIQUES
3-Needle Bind-Off: With RS tog and needles parallel, using a 3rd needle, knit tog a st from the front needle with 1 from the back. *Knit tog a st from the front and back needles, and

slip the first st over the 2nd to bind off. Rep from * across, then fasten off last st.

3-St I-Cord: Cast on 3 sts. *K3, do not turn, slip sts back to LH needle; rep from * until cord is desired length. Bind off.

PATTERN NOTE
Sweater is worked with 2 strands of yarn held together throughout.

BODY
Using 2 strands of yarn throughout, cast on 157 (172, 187, 205, 220) sts and work in Welted Rib pat until piece measures 17½ (18, 18½, 18 ½, 19) inches, ending with a WS row.

Divide for armholes
Next row (RS): Work across 41 (45, 48, 53, 57) front sts and place on holder; work across 76 (82, 91, 100, 106) back sts; place rem 40 (45, 48, 52, 57) sts on another holder.

BACK
Work 1 WS row.

Bind off 0 (0, 0, 3, 4) sts at beg of next 2 rows—76 (82, 91, 94, 98) sts.

Dec row (RS): K1, ssk, work to last 3 sts, k2tog, k1—74 (80, 89, 92, 96) sts.

Next row: P2, work to last 2 sts, p2.

Maintaining established pat and working first and last st in St st, rep last 2 rows 11 (12, 13, 14, 15) times—52 (56, 63, 64, 66) sts.

Work even until armholes measure 8 (8½, 9, 9½, 10) inches, ending with a WS row.

Next row (RS): Work 12 (14, 16, 16, 18) sts and place these sts on holder for shoulder; bind off center 28 (28, 31, 32, 30) back neck sts; work rem 12 (14, 16, 16, 18) shoulder sts and place on another holder.

RIGHT FRONT
Row 1: With WS facing, rejoin yarn; bind off 1 (0, 0, 3, 5) st(s), work to end—40 (45, 48, 50, 52) sts.

Dec row (RS): Work to last 3 sts, k2tog, k1—39 (44, 47, 49, 51) sts.

Next row (WS): P2, work to end.

Maintaining established pat, rep last 2 rows 11 (12, 13, 14, 15) times—28 (32, 34, 35, 36) sts.

Work even until armhole measures 5 (5½, 6, 61/2, 7) inches, ending with a RS row.

Shape neck
Shape neck with short rows as follows:

Row 1 (WS): Work across 20 (24, 26, 27, 28) sts, W&T.

Rows 2, 4, 6 and 8: Work to end of row.

Row 3: Work across 16 (20, 22, 23, 24) sts, W&T.

Row 5: Work across 14 (18, 20, 21, 22) sts, W&T.
Row 7: Work across 12 (16, 18, 19, 20) sts, W&T.
Row 9: Work to end of row.
Row 10: Bind off 16 (18, 18, 19, 18) sts, work to end—12 (14, 16, 16, 18) sts.

Work even until front measures same as back.

Place sts on holder.

LEFT FRONT

Row 1: With RS facing, rejoin yarn; bind off 0 (0, 0, 2, 5) sts, work to end—40 (45, 48, 50, 52) sts.

Work 1 row even.

Dec row (RS): K1, ssk, work to end of row.
Next row: Work to last 2 sts, p2.

Rep last 2 rows 11 (12, 13, 14, 15) times—28 (28, 34, 35, 36) sts.

Work even until armhole measures 5 (5½, 6, 6½, 7) inches, ending with a WS row.

Shape neck

Shape neck with short rows as follows:
Row 1 (RS): Work across 20 (24, 26, 27, 28) sts, W&T.
Rows 2, 4, 6 and 8: Work to end of row.
Row 3: Work across 16 (20, 22, 23, 24) sts, W&T.
Row 5: Work across 14 (18, 20, 21, 22) sts, W&T.
Row 7: Work across 12 (16, 18, 19, 20) sts, W&T.
Row 9: Work to end of row.
Row 10: Bind off 16 (18, 18, 19, 18) sts, work to end of row—12 (14, 16, 16, 18) sts.

Work even until front measures same as back.
Place sts on holder.

SLEEVES

Using 2 strands of yarn, cast on 37 (37, 37, 46, 46) sts.

Work 9 (8, 7, 9, 8) rows in Welted Rib pat.

Inc row: Maintaining first and last (selvedge) sts in St st, work 1 st, M1R, work in established pat, M1L, work 1 st—39 (39, 39, 48, 48) sts.

Working new sts into pat as they accumulate, rep Inc row every 10 (9, 8, 10, 9) rows 9 (11, 13, 10, 12) times—57 (61, 65, 68, 72) sts.

Work even until piece measures 17 (18, 19, 19, 20) inches or desired length, ending with a WS row.

Dec row (RS): K1, ssk, work to last 3 sts, k2tog, k1.
Next row: P2, work to last 2 sts, p2.

Maintaining established pat, rep last 2 rows 11 (12, 13, 14, 15) times—33 (35, 37, 38, 40) sts.
Bind off.

FINISHING

Weave in all ends.
Block pieces to finished measurements.
Join shoulders using 3-Needle Bind-Off.
Sew in sleeves; sew sleeve seams.

I-CORD CLOSURES

Using dpns and 1 strand of yarn, make 3 I-cords, each approx 20 inches long.

Sew I-cord in a clover leaf design (see photo), then attach to coat.

Sew buttons opposite I-cord closures. ●

ENCHANTED FOREST **SCHEMATICS**

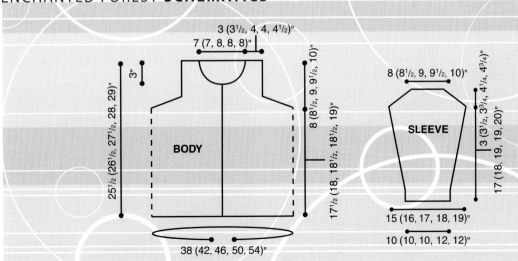

BOHEMIAN**rhapsody**

DESIGN BY ANN WEAVER

Modeled after a man's tailored suit jacket, this piece incorporates edgy details into a classic shape.

◼◼◼◼ EXPERIENCED

SIZES

Woman's extra-small (small, medium, large, extra-large, 2X-large) Instructions are given for smallest size, with larger sizes in parentheses. When only 1 number is given, it applies to all sizes.

FINISHED MEASUREMENTS

Chest: 33½ (36½, 39½, 44, 47, 51½) inches (buttoned)
Length to shoulders: 20¾ (21¼, 22¼, 23½, 24½, 25¼) inches

MATERIALS

Berroco Peruvia (heavy worsted weight; 100% Peruvian highland wool; 174 yds/100g per hank): 6 (6, 7, 8, 9, 10) hanks peat moss #7141 (MC); 1 skein vino tinto #7153 (CC)

4 MEDIUM

Size 9 (5.5mm) 40-inch circular needle or size needed to obtain gauge
2 stitch holders
Stitch markers
Sewing needle
Sewing thread to match MC
4 (1-inch) buttons

GAUGE

16 sts and 22 rows = 4 inches in St st.
To save time, take time to check gauge.

SPECIAL ABBREVIATIONS

Place marker (pm): Place a marker to separate sections.
Slip marker (sm): Slip marker when you come to it.
Knit in front and back of stitch (kfb): Inc by knitting in front loop, then in back loop of st.
Purl in front and back of stitch (pfb): Inc by purling in front loop, then in back loop of st.
Left-Leaning Double Decrease on WS (sssp): Slip next 3 sts one at a time kwise, pass back to LH needle and p3tog-tbl.

SPECIAL TECHNIQUE

2-Row Buttonhole
Row 1 (RS): K3, bind off 3, work to end of row as indicated.
Row 2: Work to last 6 sts, cast on 3, p3.

PATTERN STITCH

Woven Pat (multiple of 3 sts)
Row 1 (RS): Carrying CC without knitting it, *sl 2 wyif, sl 1 wyib; rep from * across.
Row 2: Carrying CC without knitting it, *sl 1 wyif, sl 2 wyib; rep from * across.
Rows 3–8: With MC, work in St st.
Row 9: Carrying CC without knitting it, *sl 2 wyib, sl 1 wyif; rep from * across.
Row 10: Carrying CC without knitting it, *sl 1 wyib, sl 2 wyif; rep from * across.
Rows 11–16: With MC, work in St st.
 Rep Rows 1–16 for pat, carrying CC loosely up side of work.

PATTERN NOTES

This jacket is worked in 1 piece from the bottom up and has waist and lapel shaping; buttonholes are worked in the main fabric.

The body is divided at the armholes into fronts and back. Sleeves are worked back and forth from the bottom up.

The garment is meant to fit with approximately 2 inches of positive ease.

When working Rows 1, 2, 9 and 10 of the Woven pattern, you will not actually knit with the CC yarn. The color is woven back and forth between slipped stitches.

BODY

With CC, cast on 38 (44, 47, 50, 53, 56) right front sts, pm for side seam, cast on 67 (73, 79, 88, 94, 103) back sts, pm for side seam, cast on 38 (44, 47, 50, 53, 56) left front sts—143 (161, 173, 188, 200, 215) sts.

Row 1 (RS): With CC, knit, cut CC.
Row 2: Join MC and knit.
Row 3: *K1, p1; rep from * across.

Beg with purl row, work in St st until body measures 3 (3½, 3½, 3¾, 4, 4) inches, ending with a WS row.

Buttonholes and waist shaping

Dec row (RS): Work buttonhole, *knit to 2 sts before marker, ssk, sm, k2tog; rep from *, then knit to end—139 (157, 169, 184, 196, 211) sts.

Work 5 rows even, completing buttonhole on first row.

Rep Dec row, omitting buttonhole—135 (153, 165, 180, 192, 207) sts.

Work 5 rows even.

Beg Woven pat and work 2 rows.

Rep Dec row, including button hole—131 (149, 161, 176, 188, 203) sts.

Work 5 rows even, completing buttonhole on first row.

Next row (RS): Work Row 9 of Woven pat to 2 sts before first marker, sl 1 wyib, sl 1 wyif, sm; work in pat to 2 sts before 2nd marker, sl 1 wyib, sl 1 wyif, sm, sl 1 wyib, sl 1 wyif; work in pat to end of row.

Next row: Work Row 10 of pat to 2 sts before first marker; sl 1 wyif, sl 1 wyib, sm, sl 1 wyif, sl 1 wyib; work in pat to 2nd marker, sm, sl 1 wyif, sl 1 wyib; work in pat to end of row.

Work 6 rows even.

Next row (RS): Work Row 1 of pat to 2 sts before first marker; sl 1 wyif, sl 1 wyib, sm; work in pat to 2 sts before 2nd marker, sl 1 wyif, sl 1 wyib, sm, sl 1 wyif, sl 1 wyib; work in pat to end of row.

Next row: Work Row 2 of pat to 2 sts before

first marker; sl 1 wyib, sl 1 wyif, sm, sl 1 wyib, sl 1 wyif; work in pat to 2nd marker, sm, sl 1 wyib, sl 1 wyif; work in pat to end of row.

Inc row (RS): Work buttonhole, *work to 1 st before marker, kfb, sm, kfb; rep from *, work to end—135 (153, 165, 180, 192, 207) sts.

Work 7 rows even in Woven pat, completing buttonhole on first row.

Rep Inc row, omitting buttonhole—139 (157, 169, 184, 196, 211) sts.

Work 5 rows even.

Next row (RS): Work Row 1 of pat to 1 st before first marker; sl 1 wyib, sm; work in pat to 2 sts before 2nd marker, sl 1 wyif, sl 1 wyib, sm, sl 1 wyib; work in pat to end of row.

Next row: Work Row 2 of pat to 1 st before first marker; sl 1 wyib, sm, sl 1 wyib, sl 1 wyif; work in pat to 2nd marker, sm, sl 1 wyib; work in pat to end of row.

Rep Inc row, including buttonhole—143 (161, 173, 188, 200, 215) sts.

Work 3 rows even, completing buttonhole on first row.

Lapel shaping

Discontinue Woven pat; work in St st with MC.
Row 1 (RS): Kfb, work to last st, kfb—1 lapel st each side.
Row 2: K1, pm, yo, sssp, work to last 4 sts, p3tog, yo, pm, k1—1 front st dec'd each side.
Row 3: Pfb, work to last st, pfb—2 lapel sts.
Row 4: Knit to first marker, sm, yo, sssp, work to 3 sts before last marker, p3tog, yo, sm, knit to end—1 front st dec'd each side.

Rep [Rows 3 and 4] 4 (4, 5, 6, 7, 8) more times, then work Row 3 once more—7 (7, 8, 9,10, 11) lapel sts each side and 32 (38, 40, 42, 44, 46) sts each front.

Next row (WS): Work even.

RIGHT FRONT

Special lapel edge instructions

Inc Lapel (RS): Pfb, work to end of row.
Dec Front (WS): Purl to 3 sts before marker, sssp, yo, sm, knit to end.
Work Lapel Even (RS): Work even.
Work Front Even (WS): Purl to 2 sts before marker, ssp, yo, sm, knit to end.

Row 1 (RS): Pfb, work to side seam marker; removing markers, slip back and left front sts to separate lengths of waste yarn—8 (8, 9, 10, 11, 12) lapel sts.
Row 2: Bind off 4 sts, Dec Front—27 (33, 35, 37, 39, 41) front sts.
Row 3: Inc Lapel—9 (9, 10, 11, 12, 13) lapel sts.
Row 4: Bind off 3 sts, Dec Front—23 (29, 31, 33, 35, 37) front sts.
Row 5: Work Lapel Even.
Row 6: Sl 1, p2tog, then Work Front Even—22 (28, 30, 32, 34, 36) front sts.
  Continue as follows:
  At lapel edge, work 4-row sequence of [Inc Lapel, Dec Front, Work Lapel Even, Work Front Even] 4 (5, 6, 7, 7, 8) times and *at the same time*, dec 1 st at armhole edge [every WS row] 2 (2, 2, 3, 3, 3) more times—16 (21, 22, 22, 24, 25) front sts; 12 (13, 15, 17, 18, 20) lapel sts.

Second half of lapel

Row 1 (RS): Bind off 8 (9, 11, 12, 13, 15) sts pwise, purl to marker, sm, knit to end of row—4 (4, 4, 5, 5, 5) lapel sts.
Row 2: Work Front Even.
Row 3: Inc Lapel—5 (5, 5, 6, 6, 6) lapel sts.
  Rep [Rows 2 and 3] 7 (8, 10, 11, 12, 14) times—12 (13, 15, 17, 18, 20) lapel sts.
Next row: Work Front Even.

Dec front

Row 1 (RS): Purl to marker, sm, k1 (the yo), ssk, knit to end of row—15 (20, 21, 21, 23, 24) front sts. **Row 2:** Dec Front—14 (19, 20, 20, 22, 23) front sts.
  Rep [Rows 1 and 2] 2 (4, 2, 2, 3, 2) times, then work [Row 1] 0 (1, 0, 1, 0, 1) more time(s)—10 (10, 16, 16, 16, 18) front sts.
  Continue to Work Lapel Even (RS rows) and Work Front Even (WS rows) until armhole measures 8 (8, 8½, 9, 9½, 10) inches, ending with a RS row.
  Place lapel sts on holder and work front sts only.

Shape shoulders

Row 1 (WS): Bind off 4 sts, work to end—6 (6, 12, 12, 12, 14) sts.
Row 2: Work even.
Row 3: Bind off 3 (3, 6, 6, 6, 7) sts, work to end—3 (3, 6, 6, 6, 7) sts.
Row 4: Work even.
  Bind off rem sts.

BACK

Slip back sts to needle with RS facing and rejoin yarn.
  Bind off 4 sts at beg of next 2 rows—59 (65, 71, 80, 86, 95) sts.
  Bind off 3 sts at beg of following 2 rows—53 (59, 65, 74, 80, 89) sts.
Dec row (RS): Sl 1, ssk, work to last 3 sts, k2tog, k1—51 (57, 63, 72, 78, 87) sts.
  Rep Dec row [every RS row] 2 (2, 2, 3, 3, 3) times—47 (53, 59, 66, 72, 81) sts.
  Work even until armhole measures 8 (8, 8½, 9, 9½, 10) inches, ending with a WS row.

Shape neck and shoulders

Row 1 (RS): K12 (12, 18, 18, 18, 20), join 2nd ball of yarn and bind off 23 (29, 23, 30, 36, 41) back neck sts, knit to end.
Row 2: Work both sides at once with separate balls of yarn; left back: bind off 4 shoulder sts, work to end; right back: work even.
Row 3: Right back: bind off 4 shoulder sts, work to end; left back: bind off 2 neck sts, work to end.
Row 4: Left back: bind off 3 (3, 6, 6, 6, 7) shoulder sts, work to end; right back: bind off 2 neck sts, work to end.
Row 5: Right back: bind off 3 (3, 6, 6, 6, 7) shoulder sts, work to end; left back: work even—3 (3, 6, 6, 6, 7) sts rem each side.
Row 6: Left back: bind off rem shoulder sts; right back: work even.
  Bind off rem right shoulder sts.

LEFT FRONT

Special lapel edge instructions

Inc Lapel (RS): Work to last st, pfb.
Dec Front (WS): Knit to marker, sm, yo, p3tog, purl to end.
Work Lapel Even (RS): Work even.
Work Front Even (WS): Knit to marker, sm, yo, p2tog, purl to end.
  Slip left front sts to needle with RS facing and rejoin yarn.

Row 1 (RS): Bind off 4 sts, Inc Lapel—28 (34, 36, 38, 40, 42) front sts; 8 (8, 9, 10, 11, 12) lapel sts.
Row 2: Dec Front—27 (33, 35, 37, 39, 41) front sts.
Row 3: Bind off 3 sts, Inc Lapel—24 (30, 32, 34, 36, 38) front sts; 9 (9, 10, 11, 12, 13) lapel sts.
Row 4: Dec Front—23 (29, 31, 33, 35, 37) front sts.
Row 5: Sl 1, ssp, Work Lapel Even—22 (28, 30, 32, 34, 36) front sts.
Row 6: Work Front Even.

Continue as follows:

At lapel edge, work 4-row sequence of [Inc Lapel, Dec Front, Work Lapel Even, Work Front Even] 3 (4, 5, 6, 6, 7) times, then [Inc Lapel, Dec Front, Work Lapel Even] once more, and at the same time, dec 1 st at armhole edge [every WS row] 2 (2, 2, 3, 3, 3) more times—16 (21, 22, 22, 24, 25) front sts; 12 (13, 15, 17, 18, 20) lapel sts.

Second half of lapel

Row 1 (WS): Bind off 8 (9, 11, 12, 13, 15) sts kwise, knit to marker, sm, Work Front Even—4 (4, 4, 5, 5, 5) lapel sts.
Row 2: Inc Lapel—5 (5, 5, 6, 6, 6) lapel sts.
Row 3: Work Front Even.

Rep [Rows 2 and 3] 7 (8, 10, 11, 12, 14) times—12 (13, 15, 17, 18, 20) lapel sts.

Dec front

Row 1 (RS): Knit to 3 sts before marker, k2tog, k1 (the yo), sm, purl to end—15 (20, 21, 21, 23, 24) front sts.
Row 2: Dec Front—14 (19, 20, 20, 22, 23) front sts.

Rep [Rows 1 and 2] 2 (4, 2, 2, 3, 2) times, then work [Row 1] 0 (1, 0, 1, 0, 1) more time(s)—10 (10, 16, 16, 16, 18) front sts.

Continue to Work Lapel Even (RS rows) and Work Front Even (WS rows) until armhole measures 8 (8, 8½, 9, 9½, 10) inches, ending with a WS row.

Place lapel sts on holder and work front sts only.

Shape shoulders

Row 1 (RS): Bind off 4 sts, work to end—6 (6, 12, 12, 12, 14) sts.
Row 2: Work even.
Row 3: Bind off 3 (3, 6, 6, 6, 7) sts, work to end—3 (3, 6, 6, 6, 7) sts.
Row 4: Work even.

Bind off rem sts.

BACK COLLAR

Slip right front lapel sts to needle.

Work in St st until piece measures 5½ (6, 6, 6½, 7, 7½) inches from shoulder bind-off. Keep sts on needle.

Slip left front lapel sts to needle.
Work in St st until piece measures 5½ (6, 6, 6½, 7, 7½) inches from shoulder bind-off. Keep sts on needle.

Graft 11 (12, 13, 14, 14, 15) right lapel sts to 11 (12, 13, 14, 14, 15) left lapel sts using Kitchener st.

Holding RS of back lapel and WS of body together, using mattress st and MC, sew back collar to back neck, easing extra lapel length into the neck of the body. This extra length will help your lapel lay flat.

SLEEVES

With CC, cast on 45 (48, 48, 51, 51, 54) sts.
Row 1 (RS): With CC, knit; cut CC.
Row 2: Join MC, and knit.
Row 3: *K1, p1; rep from * to end of row.

Beg with a purl row, work in St st until sleeve measures 7¼ (7½, 7½, 7¾, 7¾, 8) inches, ending with a WS row.

Work 26 rows of Woven pat.

Inc row (inc): With MC, k1, kfb, knit to last 2 sts, kfb, k1—47 (50, 50, 53, 53, 56) sts.

Continue in established Woven pat until 5 stripes are woven in, then continue in St st, *at the same time*, rep Inc row [every 8 rows] 3 times—53 (56, 56, 59, 59, 62) sts.

Work even until sleeve measures 17½ (18, 18, 18½, 18½, 19) inches, ending with a WS row.

Sleeve cap

Bind off 3 (4, 4, 4, 4, 5) sts at beg of next 2 rows—47 (48, 48, 51, 51, 52) sts.

Bind off 3 (3, 3, 3, 3, 3) sts at beg of next 2 rows—41 (42, 42, 45, 45, 47) sts.

Work 0 (0, 0, 4, 4, 4) rows even.

Dec row (RS): Sl 1, ssk, work to last 3 sts, k2tog, k1—39 (40, 40, 43, 43, 45) sts.

Rep Dec row [every 4 rows] 0 (0, 0, 0, 0, 1) time(s), then [every third row] 9 (9, 9, 9, 9, 10) times, working decs on WS rows as follows: sl 1, p2tog, work to last 3 sts, ssp, p1—21 (22, 22, 25, 25, 25) sts.

FINISHING
TRIM
Right front

With RS facing and CC, beg at lower edge and end at beg of lapel shaping, pick up and knit 26 (28, 28, 30, 32, 32) sts along front edge.

Knit 1 row.

Bind off loosely; cut yarn and fasten off last st.

Left front

With RS facing and CC, beg at lapel shaping and end at lower edge, pick up and knit 26 (28, 28, 30, 32, 32) sts along front edge.

Knit 1 row.

Bind off loosely; cut yarn and fasten off last st.

Lapels

With WS facing and CC, beg at beg of lapel shaping and end at corner of lapel, pick up and knit 16 (20, 24, 28, 28, 32) sts along lower edge of left lapel.

Knit 1 row.

Bind off loosely, leaving last st on needle.

Pick up and knit 7 (8, 8, 9, 9, 10) sts along top edge of left lapel, ending at corner where lapel beg to flare outward again.

Knit 1 row.

Bind off loosely, leaving last st on needle.

Pick up and knit 38 (41, 41, 45, 49, 53) sts along back collar, ending at top edge of right lapel.

Knit 1 row.

Bind off loosely, leaving last st on needle.

Pick up and knit 7 (8, 8, 9, 9, 10) sts along top edge of right lapel, ending at lapel point.

Knit 1 row.

Bind off loosely, leaving last st on needle.

Pick up and knit 16 (20, 24, 28, 28, 32) sts along lower edge of right lapel, beg at top of lapel and end at beg of lapel shaping (where the trim of the right front ends).

Knit 1 row.

Bind off loosely and fasten off.

Weave in ends. Block all pieces to finished measurements.

With MC, sew shoulder seams; set in sleeves; sew sleeve seams.

Using thread in color matching MC, sew on buttons opposite buttonholes.

Try on jacket before sewing buttons in place to assure the best fit across the bust.

With MC, tack edge of back collar to back of jacket body at shoulder seams and at 2 or 3 points across back to assure it lays flat.

Steam or wet block finished jacket to relax and flatten seams. ●

BOHEMIAN RHAPSODY SCHEMATICS

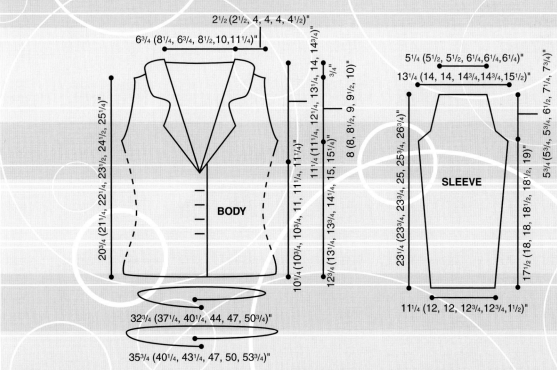

BUILD**a**FOUNDATION
fromTHE**bottom**-UP

Let's bump it up a notch and explore the endless possibilities that seamless in-the-round knitting offers. Once you master this chapter, you'll understand why the legendary Elizabeth Zimmermann often referred to circular needles as her "Particular Pets." In *Knitting Without Tears*, she opened us up to a vast world of knitting seamless sweaters created on circular needles.

SPECIAL ways OF working

With our foundation in place, it's time to move into new territory. In many respects, working a seamless garment is easier than flat back and forth knitting. One obvious reason is the lack of sewing involved. If sewing isn't your forte, or you don't feel confident in your finishing abilities, then in the round knitting is the perfect solution. How many unfinished sweaters do you have in your closet?

Gauge

Don't be tempted to jump right in without checking your gauge! It's a critical component to successful garment construction and should never be overlooked. When it comes to knitting in the round, gauge is not the same as when knitting a flat garment. The reason for this is that a knitter's tension is usually different when purling than when knitting. Also, knitting circularly can change the yardage consumed for a given project.

Make the Swatch

The Bottom-Up method is usually the simplest because unlike top-down construction which involves neck shaping at the very beginning, bottom-up construction starts with at the bottom of the garment, which usually requires very little, or no, shaping. The best way to visualize your garment is to imagine a cylindrical tube. Knitting in the round is a seamless method of working a circular garment like a pullover. But before we build upon the concept of the tube, it's important to understand the fundamentals of casting on.

Casting Onto a Circular Needle

Step One: After casting on the required number of stitches, place your work down on a flat surface, making sure the cast-on edge faces the center as indicated by the arrows. This will ensure that your stitches do not twist around the needle.

Step Two: Join the work by placing a marker on the right-hand needle so that you'll remember the location of the beginning of the round. Then, knit into the first stitch that you cast on, creating a "ring."

Working on Double-Point Needles

Most projects in this book are worked on circular needles for comfort and ease, but in some cases, projects may call for double-point needles for the following reasons: either you're working small circumference pieces, or you've decreased several stitches which creates a smaller circumference, or your circular needle is too long to accommodate your stitches. Refer to page 169 for a detailed explanation for working with double-point needles.

Working "The Tube"

Jacob's Ladder, on page 64, clearly utilizes the "tube" concept, but takes things a step further by adding new elements, such as sleeves and a yoke, which can be seen illustrated below. Directional arrows indicate that this piece is knitted from the bottom-up to the armhole, with the sleeves knitted in the round, then joined to the body. All the pieces are then joined and knit together to form the yoke, ending with the neck.

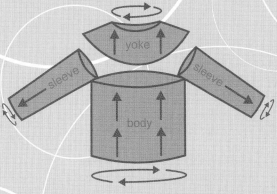

> **HOW TO** When working your first round, to keep your stitches from twisting around the needle, try using several clothespins to hold the stitches in place, removing them as you work. Or, work one row before joining into a circle. When you're done, sew the small opening closed.

WOODLAND**rose**TUNIC

DESIGN BY JEAN CLEMENT

Soft, feminine and flattering—this light and airy tunic is the perfect companion to wear with your favorite jeans or skirt.

◼◼◼◻ EXPERIENCED

SIZES
Woman's small (medium, large, extra-large, 2X-large) Instructions are given for smallest size, with larger sizes in parentheses. If only 1 number is given, it applies to all sizes.

FINISHED MEASUREMENTS
Chest: 36½ (40¾, 44½, 48¾, 52½) inches
Length: 22 (22¾, 24½, 26½, 28¼) inches

MATERIALS
Elsebeth Lavold Silky Wool (DK weight; 45% wool/35% silk/20% nylon; 192 yds/50g per ball): 4 (5, 5, 6, 6) balls acorn #62

3 LIGHT

Size 5 (3.75 mm) 16-inch circular needle
Size 7 (4.5 mm) 32-inch (or longer) circular needle or size needed to obtain gauge
Stitch markers, 1 in CC for beg of rnd
Split-ring marker (optional)
Row counter (optional)

GAUGE
21 sts and 30 rnds/rows = 4 inches/10cm in St st with larger needle.
To save time, take time to check gauge.

SPECIAL ABBREVIATIONS
S2KP2: Slip 2 sts tog kwise, k1, pass the 2 slipped sts over; a centered double-dec.
Sssk: Slip next 3 sts 1 at a time kwise, then k3tog; a left-leaning double dec.
Left Twist (LT): Slip 2 sts individually kwise and return to left needle in new orientation; knit 2nd tbl without dropping, k2tog-tbl.
Left Twist Decrease (LT-Dec): Slip 3 sts individually kwise, return to LH needle in new orientation; knit 2nd and 3rd sts tog-tbl without dropping, then k3tog-tbl.
Left Twist Increase (LT-Inc): Slip 2 sts individually kwise and return to LH needle in new orientation; knit 2nd st tbl without dropping, yo, k2tog-tbl
Right Twist (RT): K2tog, but do not drop; knit first st again.
Right Twist Decrease (RT-Dec): K3tog, but do not drop; knit first 2 sts tog again.
Right Twist Increase (RT-Inc): K2tog, but do not drop; yo, knit first st again
Place marker (pm): Place a marker on needle to separate sections.

PATTERN STITCHES
Fleurette Lace (multiple of 6 sts in the round)
   Note: St count increases on Rnds 4 and 10, returns to original count on Rnds 6 and 12.
Rnd 1 and all odd-number rnds: Knit.
Rnd 2: *K1, yo, ssk, k1, k2tog, yo; rep from * around.
Rnd 4: K2, *yo, k3; rep from * to last st, yo, k1.
Rnd 6: *S2KP2, yo, ssk, k1, k2tog, yo; rep from * around.
Rnd 8: *K1, k2tog, yo, k1, yo, ssk; rep from * around.
Rnd 10: K2, *yo, k3; rep from * to last st, yo, k1.
Rnd 12: *K1, k2tog, yo, S2KP2, yo, ssk; rep from * around.
   Rep Rnds 1–12 for pat.
Fleurette Lace (multiple of 6 sts + 3 in rows)
   Note: St count increases on Rows 4 and 10, returns to original count on Rows 6 and 12.
Row 1 and all WS rows: Purl.
Row 2 (RS): K2, *yo, ssk, k1, k2tog, yo, k1; rep from * to last st, k1.
Row 4: K2, *k1, yo, k3, yo, k2; rep from * to last st, k1.
Row 6: K1, k2tog, *yo, ssk, k1, k2tog, yo, S2KP2;

rep from * to last 8 sts, yo, ssk, k1, k2tog, yo, ssk, k1.

Row 8: K2, *k2tog, yo, k1, yo, ssk, k1; rep from * to last st, k1.

Row 10: K2, *k1, yo, k3, yo, k2; rep from * to last st, k1.

Row 12: K2, *k2tog, yo, S2KP2, yo, ssk, k1; rep from * to last st, k1.

Rep Rows 1–12 for pat.

Rosebud Pat (multiple of 12 sts)

Rnd 1 and all odd-number rnds: Knit.

Rnd 2: K7, [k2tog, yo, k1, yo, ssk, k7] 8 (8, 9,10, 11) times.

Rnd 4: K4, [k2tog, yo, k3, yo, ssk, k5] 7 (7, 8, 9, 10) times, k2tog, yo, k3, yo, ssk, k4.

Rnd 6: K4, [yo, ssk, yo, k3tog, yo, k7] 7 (7, 8, 9, 10) times, yo, ssk, yo, k3tog, yo, k4.

Rnd 8: K3, [yo, S2KP2, yo, k9] 7 (7, 8, 9, 10) times, yo, S2KP2, yo, k3.

Rnd 10: K7, [k2tog, yo, k1, yo, ssk, k7] 7 (7, 8, 9, 10) times.

Rnd 12: K4, [k2tog, yo, k3, yo, k5] 6 (6, 7, 8, 9) times, k2tog, yo, k3, yo, ssk, k4.

Rnd 14: K4, [yo, ssk, yo, k3tog, yo, k7] 6 (6, 7, 8, 9) times, yo, ssk, yo, k3tog, yo, k4.

Rnd 16: K3, [yo, S2KP2, yo, k9] 6 (6, 7, 8, 9) times, yo, S2KP2, yo, k3.

Rep Rnds 1–16 for pat.

SPECIAL TECHNIQUE

3-Needle Bind-Off: With RS tog and needles parallel, using a 3rd needle, knit tog a st from the front needle with 1 from the back. *Knit tog a st from the front and back needles, and slip the first st over the 2nd to bind off. Rep from * across, then fasten off last st.

PATTERN NOTES

This garment is worked in the round in 1 piece from the bottom up to the armholes, after which back and fronts are worked back and forth.

Rosebud pattern is worked on the front only, between lines of traveling twisted stitches; back is worked in stockinette stitch between traveling twisted stitches. Shaping decreases/increases are "hidden" within the twisted stitches. On even-numbered rounds without decreases, work a traveling left or right twist to maintain the traveling stitch detail.

A chart for Fleurette Lace pattern is provided for those preferring to work from charts.

A row counter is helpful when working this pattern.

TUNIC

BORDER

With larger needle, cast on 114 (120, 132, 144, 156) sts, pm, cast on 114 (120, 132, 144, 156) sts; pm for beg of rnd and join, taking care not to twist sts—228 (240, 264, 288, 312) sts.

Purl 1 rnd.

Work 2 reps of 12-rnd Fleurette Lace pat.

Knit 1 rnd, purl 1 rnd.

BODY

Size small

Rnd 1 and all odd number rnds: Knit.

Rnd 2 (dec): K3, LT-Dec, work Rosebud pat over 103 sts, RT-Dec, k5, LT-Dec, k103, RT-Dec, k2—224 sts.

Rnd 4 (dec): K4, LT-Dec, Rosebud pat over 99 sts, RT-Dec, k7, LT-Dec, k99, RT-Dec, k3—220 sts.

Rnd 6: K5, LT, work Rosebud pat over 97 sts, RT, k9, LT, k97, RT, k4.

Rnd 8 (dec): K6, LT-Dec, Rosebud pat over 93 sts, RT-Dec, k11, LT-Dec, k93, RT-Dec, k5—216 sts.

Rnd 10: K7, LT, work Rosebud pat over 91 sts, RT, k13, LT, k91, RT, k6.

Rnd 12 (dec): K8, LT-Dec, work Rosebud pat over 87 sts, RT-Dec, k15, LT-Dec, k87, RT-Dec, k7—212 sts.

Rnd 14: K9, LT, work Rosebud pat over 85 sts, RT, k17, LT, k85, RT, k8.

Rnd 16 (dec): K10, LT-Dec, work Rosebud pat over 81 sts, RT-Dec, k19, LT-Dec, k81, RT-Dec, k9—208 sts.

Continue as established for 32 more rnds; on each succeeding rnd, work 1 more knit st before LTs and after RTs, and work a decreasing number of sts in Rosebud pat (on front) and St st (on back) between LTs and RTs, working decs on Rnds 20, 24, 28, 32, 36, 40 and 44; on Rnd 48, dec on the front only—178 sts.

Size medium

Rnd 1 and all odd-number rnds: Knit.

Rnd 2 (dec): K6, LT-Dec, work Rosebud pat over 103 sts, RT-Dec, k11, LT-Dec, k103, RT-Dec, k5—236 sts.

Rnd 4: K7, LT, work Rosebud pat over 101 sts, RT, k13, LT, k101, RT, k6.

Rnd 6: K8, LT, work Rosebud pat over 99 sts, RT, k15, LT, k99, RT, k7.

Rnd 8 (dec): K9, LT-Dec, work Rosebud pat over 95 sts, RT-Dec, k17, LT-Dec, k95, RT-Dec, k8—232 sts.

Rnd 10: K10, LT, work Rosebud pat over 93 sts,

RT, k19, LT, k93, RT, k9.

Rnd 12: K11, LT, work Rosebud pat over 91 sts, RT, k21, LT, k91, RT, k10.

Rnd 14: K12, LT, work Rosebud pat over 89 sts, RT, k23, LT, k89, RT, k11.

Rnd 16 (dec): K13, LT-Dec, work Rosebud pat over 85 sts, RT-Dec, k25, LT-Dec, k85, RT-Dec, k12—228 sts.

Continue as established for 32 more rnds; on each succeeding rnd, work 1 more knit st before LTs and after RTs, and work a decreasing number of sts in Rosebud pat (on front) and St st (on back) between LTs and RTs, working decs on Rnds 20, 28, 32, 36, 40, 44 and 48—200 sts.

Size large
Rnd 1 and all odd number rnds: Knit.

Rnd 2 (dec): K6, LT-Dec, work Rosebud pat over 115 sts, RT-Dec, k11, LT-Dec, k115, RT-Dec, k5—260 sts.

Rnd 4: K7, LT, work Rosebud pat over 113 sts, RT, k13, LT, k113, RT, k6.

Rnd 6: K8, LT, work Rosebud pat over 111 sts, RT, k15, LT, k111, RT, k7.

Rnd 8 (dec): K9, LT-Dec, work Rosebud pat over 107 sts, RT-Dec, k17, LT-Dec, k107, RT-Dec, k8—256 sts.

Rnd 10: K10, LT, work Rosebud pat over 105 sts, RT, k19, LT, k105, RT, k9.

Rnd 12 (dec): K11, LT-Dec, work Rosebud pat over 101 sts, RT-Dec, k21, LT-Dec, k101, RT-Dec, k10—252 sts.

Rnd 14: K12, LT, work Rosebud pat over 99 sts, RT, k23, LT, k99, RT, k11.

Rnd 16 (dec): K13, LT-Dec, work Rosebud pat over 95 sts, RT-Dec, k25, LT-Dec, k95, RT-Dec, k12—248 sts.

Continue as established for 40 more rnds; on each succeeding rnd, work 1 more knit st before LTs and after RTs, and work a decreasing number of sts in Rosebud pat (on front) and St st (on back) between LTs and RTs, working decs on Rnds 24, 28, 32, 40, 44, 48 and 56—220 sts.

Size extra-large
Rnd 1 and all odd-number rnds: Knit.

Rnd 2 (dec): K6, LT-Dec, work Rosebud pat over 127 sts, RT-Dec, k11, LT-Dec, k127, RT-Dec, k5—284 sts.

Rnd 4 (dec): K7, LT-Dec, work Rosebud pat over 123 sts, RT-Dec, k13, LT-Dec, k123, RT-Dec, k6—280 sts.

Rnd 6: K8, LT, work Rosebud pat over 121 sts,

RT, k15, LT, k121, RT, k7.

Rnd 8 (dec): K9, LT-Dec, work Rosebud pat over 117 sts, RT-Dec, k17, LT-Dec, k117, RT-Dec, k8—276 sts.

Rnd 10: K10, LT, work Rosebud pat over 115 sts, RT, k19, LT, k115, RT, k9.

Rnd 12 (dec): K11, LT-Dec, work Rosebud pat over 111 sts, RT-Dec, k21, LT-Dec, k111, RT-Dec, k10—272 sts.

Rnd 14: K12, LT, work Rosebud pat over 109 sts, RT, k23, LT, k109, RT, k11.

Rnd 16 (dec): K13, LT-Dec, work Rosebud pat over 105 sts, RT-Dec, k25, LT-Dec, k105, RT-Dec, k12—268 sts.

Continue as established for 48 more rnds; on each succeeding rnd, work 1 more knit st before LTs and after RTs, and work a decreasing number of sts in Rosebud pat (on front) and St st (on back) between LTs and RTs, working decs on Rnds 24, 28, 32, 40, 44 and 48; on Rnd 56, dec on the front only—242 sts.

Size 2X-large
Rnd 1 and all odd-number rnds: Knit.

Rnd 2 (dec): K6, LT-Dec, work Rosebud pat over 139 sts, RT-Dec, k11, LT-Dec, k139, RT-Dec, k5—308 sts.

Rnd 4: K7, LT, work Rosebud pat over 135 sts, RT, k13, LT, k135, RT, k6.

Rnd 6: K8, LT, work Rosebud pat over 133 sts, RT, k15, LT, k133, RT, k7.

Rnd 8 (dec): K9, LT-Dec, work Rosebud pat over 129 sts, RT-Dec, k17, LT-Dec, k129, RT-Dec, k8—304 sts.

Rnd 10: K10, LT, work Rosebud pat over 127 sts, RT, k19, LT, k127, RT, k9.

Rnd 12 (dec): K11, LT-Dec, work Rosebud pat over 123 sts, RT-Dec, k21, LT-Dec, k123, RT-Dec, k10—300 sts.

Rnd 14: K12, LT, work Rosebud pat over 121 sts, RT, k23, LT, k121, RT, k11.

Rnd 16 (dec): K13, LT-Dec, work Rosebud pat over 117 sts, RT-Dec, k25, LT-Dec, k117, RT-Dec, k12—296 sts.

Continue as established for 56 more rnds; on each succeeding rnd, work 1 more knit st before LTs and after RTs, and work a decreasing number of sts in Rosebud pat (on front) and St st (on back) between LTs and RTs, working decs on Rnds 24, 32, 36, 40, 48, 56, 60 and 64; on Rnd 72, dec on the front only—262 sts.

All Sizes

Next rnd: Knit.

Next rnd: Work pat as established with left/right twisted sts.

Next rnd: Knit.

Next rnd (inc): Knit to twisted sts, LT-Inc, work Rosebud pat over 27 sts, RT-Inc, knit to next twisted sts, LT-Inc, k27, RT-Inc, knit to end of rnd—182 (204, 224, 246, 266) sts.

Next 3 rnds: Work even with left/right twisted sts on 2nd rnd.

Next rnd (inc front only): Knit to twisted sts, LT-Inc, work Rosebud pat over 23 sts, RT-Inc, knit to next twisted sts, LT, k23, RT, knit to end of rnd—184 (206, 226, 248, 268) sts.

Next 3 rnds: Work even with left/right twisted sts on 2nd rnd.

Next rnd (inc): Knit to twisted sts, LT-Inc, work Rosebud pat over 19 sts, RT-Inc, knit to next twisted sts, LT-Inc, k19, RT-Inc, knit to end of rnd—188 (210, 230, 252, 272) sts.

Next 3 rnds: Work even with left/right twisted sts on 2nd rnd.

Next rnd (inc): Knit to twisted sts, LT-Inc, work Rosebud pat over 15 sts, RT-Inc, knit to next twisted sts, LT-Inc, k15, RT-Inc, knit to end of rnd—192 (214, 234, 256, 276) sts.

Next rnd: Knit.

Next rnd: Knit to twisted sts, LT, knit to twisted sts, RT, knit to twisted sts, LT, knit to twisted sts, RT, knit to end of rnd.

Next rnd: Knit.

Rep [last 2 rnds] 4 more times.

Work 4 more rnds working left/right twisted sts every rnd as you come to them; on the final rnd, work twisted sts as follows: LT leaving 2nd st on needle, slip st to left needle and work RT—192 (214, 234, 256, 276) sts.

Next rnd: Purl.

Divide for back and fronts

Transfer the first 97 (107, 117, 127, 139) sts to waste yarn to hold for fronts.

BACK

Note: Do not count yo's on Rows 4 and 10 when counting sts.

Row 1 and all WS rows: Purl.

Row 2 [sizes small (medium, 2X-large, first rep only] (dec): K2, ssk, [yo, ssk, k1, k2tog, yo, k1] 14 (16, 21) times, yo, ssk, k1, k2tog, k2—93 (105, --, --, 135) sts.

Row 2 [sizes large, extra large; all reps all sizes]: K2, [yo, ssk, k1, k2tog, yo, k1] 14 (16, 18, 20, 21) times, yo, ssk, k1, k2tog, yo, k2.

Row 4: K2, [k1, yo, k3, yo, k2] 15 (17, 19, 21, 22) times, k1.

Row 6: K1, k2tog [yo, ssk, k1, k2tog, yo, S2KP2] 14 (16, 18, 20, 21) times, yo, ssk, k1, k2tog, yo, ssk, k1.

Row 8: K2, [k2tog, yo, k1, yo, ssk, k1] 15 (17, 19, 21, 22) times, k1.

Row 10: Rep Row 4.

Row 12: K2 [k2tog, yo, S2KP2, yo, ssk, k1] 15, (17, 19, 21, 22) times, k1.

Rep [Rows 1–12] 4 (4, 5, 5, 6) times, then work [Rows 1–6] 0 (1, 0, 1, 0) time(s).

Next row (WS): Purl.

Next row (RS): K30 (34, 39, 43, 45); turn, leaving rem sts unworked.

Next row: Purl to end of row.

Next row: K30 (34, 39, 43, 45) and place on waste yarn for shoulder; bind off center 33 (37, 39, 43, 45) back neck sts; knit to end of row.

Next row: Purl.

Next row: Knit, then place sts on waste yarn for shoulder.

RIGHT FRONT

With WS of front facing, place 1 (1, 0, 0, 1) st(s) on holder, join yarn and p47 (52, 58, 63, 68), leaving rem sts on holder for left front.

Set-up Fleurette Lace pat on next row as follows:

Small: K1, ssk, [yo, ssk, k1, k2tog, yo, k1] 6 times, yo, ssk, k1, k2tog, yo, k2tog, k1—45 sts.

Medium: K1, ssk, [yo, ssk, k1, k2tog, yo, k1] 7 times, yo, ssk, k1, k2tog, k2—50 sts.

Large: K1, ssk, [yo, ssk, k1, k2tog, yo, k1] 8 times, yo, ssk, k1, k2tog, k2—56 sts.

Extra-large: K1, ssk, [yo, ssk, k1, k2tog, yo, k1] 9 times, yo, ssk, k1, k2tog, k1—61 sts.

2X-large: K1, ssk, [yo, ssk, k1, k2tog, yo, k1] 10 times, yo, ssk, k2tog, k1—66 sts.

Continue in Fleurette Lace pat as established and *at the same time*, dec 1 st at neck edge as established [every 4 rows] 12 (16, 17, 18, 20) times, then [every 3 rows] 3 (0, 0, 0, 1) times, maintaining pat as much as possible and working neck sts in St st when there are insufficient sts to work corresponding yo and dec (*Note:* On Rows 18, 24 and 66 work neck edge dec and pat dec at once as sssk to maintain pat)—30 (34, 39, 43, 45) sts.

After completing 60 (66, 72, 78, 84) rows, place sts on holder.

LEFT FRONT

With WS facing, place 1 st for center front on holder, join yarn and p47 (52, 58, 63, 68).

Set-up Fleurette Lace pat on next row as follows:

Small: K1, ssk, [yo, ssk, k1, k2tog, yo, k1] 6 times, yo, ssk, k1, k2tog, yo, k2tog, k1—45 sts.

Medium: K2, [ssk, k1, k2tog, yo, k1, yo] 7 times, ssk, k1, k2tog, yo, k2tog, k1—50 sts.

Large: K2, [ssk, k1, k2tog, yo, k1, yo] 8 times, ssk, k1, k2tog, yo, k2tog, k1—56 sts.

Extra-large: K1, ssk, [k1, k2tog, yo, k1, yo, ssk] 9 times, k1, k2tog, yo, k2tog, k1—61 sts.

2X-large: K1, ssk, [k2tog, yo, k1, yo, ssk, k1] 10 times, k2tog, yo, k2tog, k1—66 sts.

Continue in Fleurette Lace pat as established and *at the same time*, dec 1 st at neck edge as established [every 4 rows] 12 (16, 17, 18, 20) times, then [every 3 rows] 3 (0, 0, 0, 1) times, maintaining pat as much as possible and working neck sts in St st when there are insufficient sts to work corresponding yo and dec (**Note:** *On Rows 18, 24 and 66 work neck edge dec as k3tog to maintain pat*)—30 (34, 39, 43, 45) sts.

FINISHING

Join front and back shoulders using 3-Needle Bind-Off.

NECK EDGING

With smaller needle, beg at left shoulder seam, pick up and knit 47 (51, 57, 61, 65) sts along left front, knit center st and mark it with split-ring marker, pick up and knit 47 (51, 57, 61, 65) sts along right front and 35 (39, 40, 44, 46) along back neck; place marker and join—130 (142, 155, 167, 177) sts.

Rnd 1: Knit to 1 st before marked center front st, S2KP2, knit to end of rnd—128 (140, 153, 165, 175) sts.

Rnd 2: Purl to 1 st before marked center front st, p3tog, purl to end of rnd—126 (138, 151, 163, 173) sts.

Bind off to 1 st before marked center front st, k3tog and bind off, bind off rem sts.

ARMHOLE EDGING

With smaller needle, beg at center underarm, place 1 (1, 0, 0, 1) held st on needle, pick up and knit 96 (104, 115, 123, 132) sts evenly spaced around armhole.

Rnd 1: Knit.

Rnd 2: Purl.

Rep for 2nd armhole.

Weave in all ends. Block to finished measurements. ●

WOODLAND ROSE TUNIC **SCHEMATIC AND CHART**

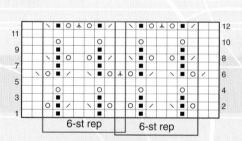

Fleurette Lace

STITCH KEY
- ☐ 6-st rep worked in the rnd; work these sts only
- ☐ 6-st rep worked back and forth; work entire chart
- ☐ K on RS, p on WS
- ■ No stitch
- ○ Yo
- ◺ Ssk
- ◹ K2tog
- ⼈ S2KP2

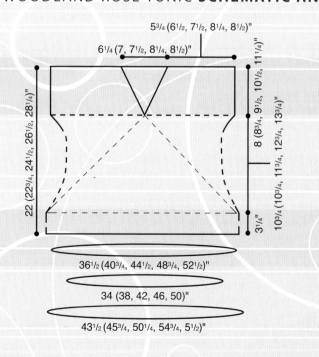

SALAMANCA**skirt**

DESIGN BY SHIRLEY MACNULTY

For a night out on the town, or a stroll in the park, this little number will turn some heads.

 EASY

SIZES
Woman's extra-small (small, medium, large) Instructions are given for the smallest size with larger sizes in parentheses. When only 1 number is given, it applies to all sizes.

FINISHED MEASUREMENTS
Waist circumference: 24½ (26¾, 30½, 34¼) inches
Bottom circumference: 46½ (50¾, 55, 59) inches
Length: 19½ (20½, 21, 21½) inches

MATERIALS
Knit One Crochet Too TY-DY Socks (sock weight; 80% wool/20% nylon; 436 yds/100g per ball): 3 (4, 4, 4) balls painted desert #1289
Size 1 (2.5mm) 24- and 32-inch circular needles or size needed to obtain gauge
Stitch markers, 1 in CC for beg of rnd
Safety pin
White sewing thread and sewing needle
Elastic band 1-inch x 25 (27, 34) inches

1 SUPER FINE

GAUGE
36 sts and 44 rnds = 4 inches/10cm in rev St st.
To save time, take time to check gauge.

SPECIAL ABBREVIATIONS
Place marker (pm): Place a marker on needle to separate sections.
Rib 10: K2 [p2, k2] twice.

PATTERN NOTES
This skirt is worked in the round from the bottom up.
　Because of the large number of stitches at the beginning, use markers to separate panels; after knitting a few inches you may remove the markers, except the beginning-of-round marker.
　Change to shorter needle when stitches no longer fit comfortably on longer needle.
　To prevent pooling of colors, it is best to work with 2 balls of yarn, changing yarns at the beginning of each round by bringing the new yarn under yarn used on previous round.

SKIRT
With 32-inch needle and using long-tail method, [cast on 38 sts, pm] 11 (12, 13, 14) times, using beg of rnd marker for last marker; join, taking care not to twist sts—418 (456, 494, 532) sts.
Rnd 1: [Rib 10, *k1, p1; rep from * to marker] 11 (12, 13, 14) times.
Rnd 2: [Rib 10, *p1, k1; rep from * to next marker] 11 (12, 13, 14) times.
Rnd 3: Rep Rnd 1.
Pat rnd: [Rib 10, purl to marker] 11 (12, 13, 14) times.
　Work even in established pat until piece measures 2 (2, 2, 3) inches.
Dec rnd: [Rib 10, p13, p2tog, p13] 11 (12, 13, 14)

times—37 sts (27 in rev St st) in each panel. Work even for 15 rnds.

Dec rnd: [Rib 10, p13, p2tog, p12] 11 (12, 13, 14) times—36 sts (26 in rev St st) in each panel.

Continue in established pat and dec 1 in the middle of each rev St st section [every 16 rnds] 0 (1, 3, 6) times, then [every 11 rnds] 14 (13, 11, 6) times—22 (22, 23, 24) sts in each panel; 242 (264, 299, 336) total sts.

Work even until piece measures approx 18½ (19½, 20, 20 ½) inches or desired length to waistband.

OUTER WAISTBAND

Waistband is worked back and forth.

Row 1 (RS): Cast on 1 st, *k2, [p2tog, k2] twice, purl to next rib section; rep from * to end, turn—221 (241, 274, 309) sts.

Row 2 (WS): *Knit to first rib, p2, [k1, p2] twice; rep from * to last st, p1.

Row 3: K1, *k2, [p1, k2] twice, purl to next rib section; rep from * to end.

Rep Rows 2 and 3 until waistband is just slightly wider than elastic, ending with a WS row.

WAISTBAND HEM

Beg with a RS row, work in St st until hem measures same as outer waistband.

Bind off.

Cut yarn, leaving a tail several inches longer than the waistband.

FINISHING

Weave in all ends except bind-off tail; block to finished measurements.

With tapestry needle and tail, whipstitch the inside of waistband to skirt along the purl rib st dec line.

Attach safety pin to one end of elastic and carefully thread band through waistband opening, using safety pin as a guide. Remove safety pin. Overlap ends of elastic for 1 inch and sew tog. Sew ends of waistband together. ●

SALAMANCA SKIRT SCHEMATIC

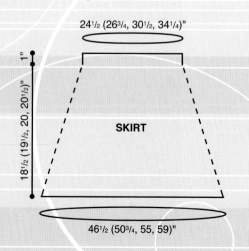

24½ (26¾, 30½, 34¼)"

1"

18½ (19½, 20, 20½)"

SKIRT

46½ (50¾, 55, 59)"

JACOB'S **ladder**

DESIGN BY ANN WEAVER

Created in the style of traditional Lopi garments, this pullover is modern, cozy and timeless.

◼◼◼▢ INTERMEDIATE

SKILL LEVEL
Intermediate

SIZES
Woman's small (medium, large, extra-large, 2X-large, 3X-large) Instructions are given for smallest size, with larger sizes in parentheses. When only 1 number is given, it applies to all sizes.

FINISHED MEASUREMENTS
Chest: 35¼ (38¾, 42, 47¼, 50½, 55½) inches
Length: 21 (22½, 24, 25½, 26¾, 28) inches

MATERIALS
The Fibre Company Terra (worsted weight; 40% baby alpaca/40% wool/20% silk; 100 yds/50g per skein): 8 (10, 11, 13, 15, 17) skeins indigo medium (MC); 1 (1, 2, 2, 3, 3) skein(s) shale (CC)
Size 5 (3.75mm) 24-inch circular needle
Size 8 (5.5mm) double-point (set of 4), 16- and 24-inch circular needles or size needed to obtain gauge
Stitch markers, 1 in CC for beg of rnd

4 MEDIUM

GAUGE
19 sts and 24 rnds = 4 inches/10cm in St st with larger needle.
To save time, take time to check gauge.

SPECIAL ABBREVIATIONS
Place marker (pm): Place a marker on needle to separate sections.
Knit in front and back of stitch (kfb): Inc by knitting in front loop, then in back loop of st.
Wrap and Turn (W&T): Bring yarn to RS of work between needles, slip next st pwise to RH needle, bring yarn around this st to WS, slip st

back to LH needle, turn work to begin working back in the other direction.

PATTERN STITCH
Waist Rib (multiple of 8 sts)
Rnd 1: *P1, k7; rep from * around.
Rnds 2 and 3: *P2, k5, p1; rep from * around.
Rnds 4–6: Rep Rnd 1.
  Rep Rnds 1–6 for pat.

SPECIAL TECHNIQUE
Hiding wraps: *On RS rows:* Pick up wrap from front to back and knit tog with wrapped st.

PATTERN NOTES
The body is made in 1 piece from the bottom up working in the round; sleeves are also worked in the round from the cuff up. Body and sleeves are then joined and yoke is in 1 piece to neck. The front neck is shaped using short rows.

When working sleeves, change to circular needle when there are enough stitches to do so; when working yoke, change to shorter needle when stitches no longer fit comfortably on longer needle.

Skeins of Terra vary in color, even within the same dye lot. To avoid obvious striping, work from 2 different skeins alternating skeins every 2 rounds.

BODY
With larger needle and MC, cast on 84 (92, 100, 112, 120, 132) back sts, pm, cast on 84 (92, 100, 112, 120, 132) front sts; pm for beg of rnd and join, taking care not to twist sts—168 (184, 200, 224, 240, 264) sts

Work K3, P1 Rib until piece measures 2 (2, 2, 3, 3, 3) inches.

Change to St st and work even until piece measures 4½ (4½, 5, 5, 5½, 6) inches.

Change to smaller needle and work 6-rnd

Waist Rib pat 5 times, the work Rnds 1–4 once more.

Change to larger needle and work in St st until piece measures 14 (14, 15, 16, 16½, 17) inches.

Next rnd: Removing markers, *work to 5 (6, 6, 6, 8, 8) sts before marker, bind off next 10 (12, 12, 12, 16, 16) sts for underarm; rep from * once—74 (80, 88, 100, 104, 116) sts each back and front.

Do not cut yarn; set needle with front and back sts aside.

SLEEVES

With larger dpns and MC, cast on 44 (44, 48, 48, 52, 52) sts and distribute sts among 3 dpns; pm for beg of rnd and join, taking care not to twist sts.

Work in K3, P1 Rib until piece measures 2 (2, 2, 3, 3, 3) inches.

Change to St st and work until piece measures 7 (7, 7, 7, 8, 8) inches.

Inc rnd: Kfb, knit to last st, kfb—46 (46, 50, 50, 54, 54) sts.

Rep Inc rnd [every 6 (6, 6, 5, 5, 4) rnds] 9 (10, 11, 14, 15, 18) times—64 (68, 72, 78, 84, 90) sts.

Work even until piece measures 17½ (18,

19, 20, 20½, 21) inches or desired length to underarm.

Next rnd: Removing marker, knit to last 5 (6, 6, 6, 8, 8) sts, bind off 10 (12, 12, 12, 16, 16) sts—54 (56, 60, 66, 68, 74) sts.

Transfer sts of first sleeve to waste yarn. Rep for 2nd sleeve, but keep sts on needle.

YOKE

Joining rnd: With MC, knit across back sts, pm, knit across 2nd sleeve sts, pm, knit across front sts, pm, transfer first sleeve sts to LH needle and knit across, pm for beg of rnd and join—256 (272, 296, 332, 344, 380) yoke sts.

Work 4 rnds even.

Set-up rnd: Knit and dec 2 (0, 0, 4, 0, 4) sts evenly across back sts [72 (80, 88, 96, 104, 112) sts between first and 2nd markers]; inc 2 (0, inc 4, dec 2, inc 4, dec 2) sts evenly across left shoulder sts [56 (56, 64, 64, 72, 72) sts between 2nd and 3rd markers]; dec 2 (0, 0, 4, 0, 4) sts evenly across front sts [72 (80, 88, 96, 104, 112) sts between 3rd and 4th markers]; inc 2 (0, inc 4, dec 2, inc 4, dec 2) sts evenly across right shoulder sts [56 (56, 64, 64, 72, 72) sts between 4th and first markers]—256 (272, 304, 320, 352, 368) total sts.

Join CC and work Rnds 1–17 of Yoke chart—192 (204, 228, 240, 264, 276) sts.

Work [Rnds 14–17] of Yoke chart 0 (1, 2, 2, 3, 3) more times.

Work Rnds 18–27 of Yoke chart—128 (136, 152, 160, 176, 184) sts.

Work [Rnds 24–27] of Yoke chart 0 (1, 1, 2, 2, 3) more times.

Work Rnds 28–33 of Yoke chart—96 (102, 114, 120, 132, 138) sts.

Next rnd: Cut MC and work with CC only; knit to 1 st before first marker, W&T.

Next rnd: Purl to 1 st before 4th marker (beg of round), W&T.

Next rnd: Knit to 5 sts before last wrapped st, W&T.

Next rnd: Purl to 5 sts before last wrapped st, W&T.

Next rnd: Knit around, hiding wraps as you come to them.

Purl 1 rnd, knit 1 rnd.

Bind off all sts kwise very loosely.

FINISHING

With MC, sew underarm sts tog.

Weave in ends. Block to finished measurements. ●

JACOB'S LADDER **SCHEMATIC AND CHART**

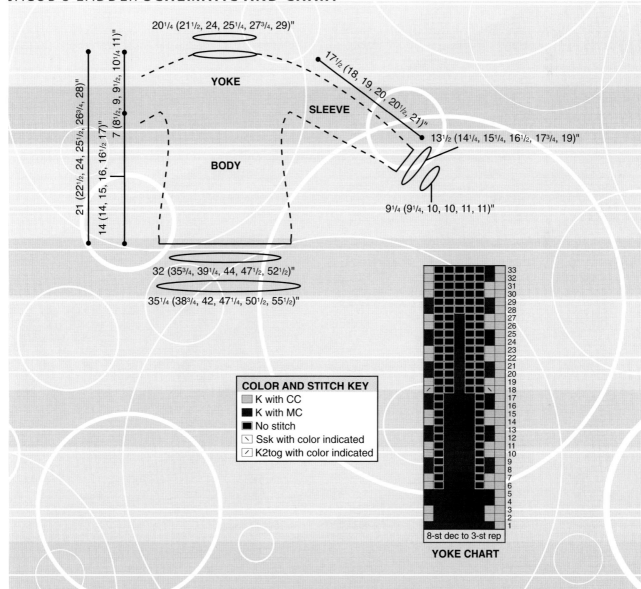

COLOR AND STITCH KEY
K with CC
K with MC
No stitch
Ssk with color indicated
K2tog with color indicated

8-st dec to 3-st rep

YOKE CHART

SHAZZAM**pullover**

DESIGN BY JEAN CLEMENT

Your kid will feel like a superhero in this pullover with pizzazz.

 INTERMEDIATE

SIZES
Child's 1 (4, 8, 12) years. Instructions are given for the smallest size, with larger sizes in parentheses. When only 1 number is given it applies to all sizes.

FINISHED MEASUREMENTS
Chest: 21¾ (26¼, 30½, 35) inches
Length: 13¼ (17¾, 20¾, 22¾) inches

MATERIALS
Patons Classic Wool (worsted weight; 100% wool; 223 yds/100g per ball): 2 (2, 3, 3) balls harvest #77236 (A), 1 (1, 2, 2) ball(s) natural mix #00229 (B)
Size 7 (4.5mm) double-point (set of 4), 16- and 24-inch circular needles
Size 8 (5mm) double-point (set of 4), 16- and 24-inch circular needles or size needed to obtain gauge
Stitch markers, 1 in CC for beg of rnd

GAUGE
22 sts and 30 rnds = 4 inches/10cm in Slip St pat with larger needle.
To save time, take time to check gauge

SPECIAL ABBREVIATIONS
Place marker (pm): Place a marker on needle to separate sections.
Slip marker (sm): Slip marker when you come to it.
Make 1 (M1): Yo on inc rnd; k1-tbl on next rnd.
Edge st: When working Zebra Chevron pat, knit with A on A rnds, and slip on B rnds. This st is used at center underarm of sleeves, and on first and last sts when working front/back yoke.

PATTERN STITCHES
Slip St pat (multiple of 6 sts)
Rnd 1: *Sl 1, k5; rep from * around.
Rnd 2: Knit.
Rep Rnds 1 and 2 for pat.
Zebra Chevron (multiple of 24 sts)
Rnds 1 and 2: With B, *sl 1, k2; rep from * around.
Rnds 3 and 4: With A, *[k2, sl 1] twice, k1, sl 1, [k2, sl 1] 3 times, k3, sl 1, k2, sl 1; rep from * around.
Rnds 5 and 6: With B, *k1, sl 1, k2, sl 1, k3, sl 1, [k2, sl 1] 3 times, k1, sl 1, k2, sl 1, k1; rep from * around.
Rnds 7 and 8: With A, rep Rnds 1 and 2.
Rnds 9 and 10: With B, rep Rnds 3 and 4.
Rnds 11 and 12: With A, rep Rnds 5 and 6.
Rep Rnds 1–12 for pat.

PATTERN NOTES
The body is worked in the round from the bottom up. After the sleeves are worked to underarm, sleeves and body are joined, and the raglan yoke is worked in one piece. The joins between body and sleeves on the first

few rounds of the yoke will be tight to work; this is normal.

This sweater is intended to have 2–4 inches of ease.

If making larger sizes, you may want to use longer circular needles.

When changing colors, always bring the new color up from under the old color to avoid holes. Carry unused yarn up the inside of garment; do not cut.

When working sleeves, change to circular needle when there are enough stitches to do so.

BODY

With smaller needle and A, cast on 60 (72, 84, 96) front sts, pm, cast on 60 (72, 84, 96) back sts; pm for beg of rnd and join, taking care not to twist sts—120 (144, 168, 192) sts.
Work 10 rnds in K1, P1 Rib.
Pat set-up rnd: Change to larger needle; k3 (0, 3, 0), work Slip St pat to last 3 (0, 3, 0) sts, sl 1 (0, 1, 0), k2 (0, 2, 0).
Continue in Slip St pat until piece measures approx 7 (10¼, 12, 13) inches, or desired length to underarm, ending with Rnd 1.
Next rnd: Knit to 5 sts past 2nd marker; removing marker, slip last 9 (11, 13, 15) sts worked to waste yarn for underarm; knit to beg

of rnd marker and slip last 4 (5, 6, 7) sts worked and first 5 (6, 7, 8) sts of rnd to waste yarn for underarm.
Leave 51 (61, 71, 81) front and back sts on needle; cut yarn and set aside.

SLEEVES

With smaller dpns and A, cast on 30 (30, 34, 34) sts; distribute sts evenly on 3 dpns; pm for beg of rnd and join, taking care not to twist sts.

Work 10 rnds in K1, P1 Rib.

Change to larger dpns and B; beg Zebra Chevron pat.

Work Zebra Chevron pat, working first st of every rnd (center underarm) as edge st and beg and end each size where indicated on chart.

Beg on Rnd 3, increase [every other rnd] 7 times, and [every 4 rnds] 8 (14, 18, 24) times, working new sts into pat as they accumulate, as follows: Edge st, M1, work in established pat to end of rnd, M1—60 (72, 84, 96) sts.

Work even (if necessary) until piece measures 9 (11½, 12½, 15½) inches or desired length, ending with Rnd 4, 8 or 12.

Cut yarn and slip sleeve sts to 2 lengths of waste yarn, with 11 (13, 15, 17) center underarm sts on one and 49 (59, 69, 79) sleeve sts on the other.

Work 2nd sleeve to match; cut yarns and slip underarm sts to waste yarn, leaving sleeve sts on 16-inch circular needle.

RAGLAN YOKE
Working first and last sts of front and back as edge sts, join sleeves to body as follows:
Joining rnd: Transfer 2nd sleeve sts to longer needle holding front and back sts; rejoin yarn to 2nd sleeve and work in established pat across sleeve, pm; slip first front st (edge st), then work in Zebra Chevron pat across front, mirroring sleeve pat across join (center front will be same st on chart as center sleeve) to last st, slip last front st (edge st), pm; transfer first sleeve sts to longer needle and work in established pat across, pm; work back as for front; pm for beg of rnd and join—200 (240, 280, 320) sts.

Work 2 rnds in established pat.
Dec rnd: *K2tog, work to last 2 sts of sleeve, ssk, sm; edge st, k2tog, work in established pat to 3 sts before marker, ssk, edge st, sm; rep from * around—192 (232, 272, 312) sts.

Next rnd: Work even.
Continue in established pat and rep last 2 rnds 14 (17, 20, 24) times; cut A—80 (96, 112, 120) sts.

Neck rib
Change to smaller 16-inch circular needle.
Working with B only, work 4 (6, 6, 6) rnds in K1, P1 Rib, knitting edge sts and working raglan decs as established—64 (72, 88, 96) sts.
Loosely bind off all sts.

FINISHING
With smaller dpn, pick up (but do not knit) 2 sts from edge of body underarm, transfer 9 (11, 13, 15) body underarm sts to dpn, pick up 2 sts from body—13 (15, 17, 19) sts.

With 2nd smaller dpn, pick up 1 st from edge of sleeve underarm, transfer 11 (13, 15, 17) sleeve underarm sts to dpn, pick up 1 st from edge of sleeve underarm—13 (15, 17, 19) sts.

With RS facing and using A, graft sts tog using Kitchener st, page 169.

Weave in ends; block to finished measurements. ●

SHAZZAM PULLOVER SCHEMATIC AND CHART

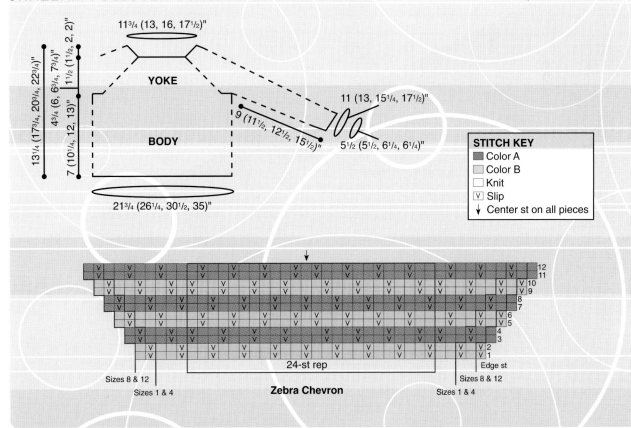

Zebra Chevron

STITCH KEY
- ▮ Color A
- ▯ Color B
- ☐ Knit
- Ⅴ Slip
- ↓ Center st on all pieces

MOM&ME**felted**BOOTIES

DESIGN BY AVA LYNNE GREEN

These cuddly booties are toasty-warm and fun to wear too!

 INTERMEDIATE

SIZES
Child's small (child's medium, child's large, woman's small, woman's medium) Instructions are given for smallest size, with larger sizes in parentheses. When only 1 number is given, it applies to all sizes.

FINISHED FELTED MEASUREMENTS
Foot length: 6 (7, 8½, 9½, 11) inches
Foot circumference: 6½ (7, 8, 9, 9½) inches
Cuff circumference: 6 (7½, 8, 8¾, 9) inches

MATERIALS
Version 1 (shown in adult size)
Brown Sheep Lamb's Pride
    Worsted (worsted weight; 85% wool/15% mohair; 190 yds/4 oz per skein): 1 (2, 2, 2, 2) skeins wild violet #M173 (A)
Brown Sheep Burly Spun (bulky weight; 100% wool; 130 yds/

4 MEDIUM

5 BULKY

8 oz per skein): 1 (1, 1, 1, 2) skeins forest floor #BS270 (B)
Version 2 (shown in child's size)
Schaefer Miss Priss (worsted weight; 100% merino wool; 280 yds/4 oz per skein): 1 (1, 1, 2, 2) skein(s) Bluebell (A)
Schaefer Esperanza (bulky weight; 70% lambswool/30% alpaca; 280 yds/8 oz per skein): 1 skein Hermione (B)
Both versions
DMC Size 3 Pearl Cotton (16 yds per skein): 1 skein each ecru, dark hunter green #3345 and topaz #725, or colors to match yarn
Size 8 (5mm) double-point needles or size needed to obtain gauge
Size 10½ (6.5mm) double-point needles or size needed to obtain gauge
Stitch markers, 1 in CC for beg of rnd
Chalk pencil
Embroidery needle

PRE-FELTING GAUGE
16 sts and 20 rnds = 4 inches/10cm in St st with smaller needles and worsted weight yarn.
10 sts and 13 rnds = 4 inches/10cm in rib with larger needles and bulky weight yarn.
Exact gauge is not critical; make sure your sts are loose and airy.

SPECIAL ABBREVIATIONS
Make 1 (M1): Insert LH needle from front to back under the running thread between the last st worked and next st on RH needle; knit into the back of resulting loop.
Place marker (pm): Place a marker to separate sections.

PATTERN NOTES
These booties are made in the round from the toe-up, with a gusset and heel flap. The ribbed cuff is knit after the foot portion is felted.

Schematic shows finished felted measurements.

BOOTIES
Toe
With smaller dpns and A, cast on 24 (28, 32, 40, 48) sts; pm for beg of rnd and join, taking care not to twist sts.
Rnd 1: Knit.
Rnd 2: *K1, M1, k10 (12, 14, 18, 22), M1, k1, pm, k1, M1, k10 (12, 14, 18, 22), M1, k1—28 (32, 36, 44, 52) sts.
Rnd 3: Knit.

Rnd 4: *K1, M1, knit to 1 st before marker, M1, k1; rep from * once—32 (36, 40, 48, 56) sts.
Rnd 5: Knit.
Rep [Rnds 4 and 5] 2 (2, 2, 2, 1) time(s)—40 (44, 48, 56, 60) sts.

FOOT
Work even until piece measures 3 (4, 5, 6, 8½) inches.

GUSSET
Rnd 1: M1, knit to marker, M1, slip marker, knit to end of rnd—42 (46, 50, 58, 62) sts.
Rnd 2: Knit.
Rep [Rnds 1 and 2] 7 (7, 8, 8, 8, 8) times—56 (60, 66, 74, 78) sts with 36 (38, 42, 46, 48) sole/gusset sts and 20 (22, 24, 28, 30) instep sts.

HEEL FLAP
Row 1 (RS): K28 (30, 33, 37, 39) sole sts, turn, leaving rem sts unworked.
Row 2: P2tog, p18 (20, 22, 26, 28), turn—19 (21, 23, 27, 29) heel flap sts.
Row 3: K2tog, k17 (19, 21, 25, 27), turn—18 (20, 22, 26, 28) heel flap sts.
Continue to work back and forth on the heel flap and dec at the beg of each row until 4 (6, 6, 10, 12) sts rem, ending with a RS row; turn.
Next row (WS, then RS): P4 (6, 6, 10, 12), do not turn; pick up and purl 8 (8, 9, 9, 9) sts down dec edge of flap, turn; sl 1, knit to other dec edge; pick up and knit 8 (8, 9, 9, 9) sts along the dec edge, turn—56 (60, 66, 74, 78) sts on all dpns.

HEEL TURN
Row 1 (WS): Sl 1, purl to slipped st, p2tog (slipped st and instep st); turn.
Row 2 (RS): Sl 1, knit to slipped st, k2tog (slipped st and instep st); turn.
Rep Rows 1 and 2 until gusset sts are used up, ending with Row 2; do not turn on last row; knit to end of rnd—42 (46, 50, 58, 62) sts rem.

ANKLE
Rnd 1: Removing gusset marker when you come to it, k20 (22, 24, 28, 30), k2tog, k18 (20, 22, 26, 28), k2tog—40 (44, 48, 56, 60) stitches.
Rnds 2–4: Knit.

Rnd 5: *Yo twice, k2tog; rep from * around.
Rnd 6: Knit around, knitting first yo and dropping the 2nd.
Rnds 7–10: Knit around.
Bind off loosely.
Weave in all ends.

FELTING
Follow basic felting instructions on page 171 until finished measurements are obtained or piece is desired size; you should no longer see individual sts. Making sure that all eyelets are open, shape the slipper into a boot, stuff and allow to dry thoroughly.

RIBBED TOP
With the crochet hook and B, *pull a loop through one of the eyelets at top of slipper, yo and pull through loop; rep from * around, placing sts on larger dpns and making sure you find all the eyelets; pm and join—20 (22, 24, 28, 30) sts.
Work K1, P1 Rib for 6 inches.
Bind off loosely in rib.

EMBROIDERY

Use a chalk pencil to lightly sketch the embroidery pat onto the toe of the slipper. Following the diagrams and using embroidery needle and pearl cotton, embroider the flower onto the toe as follows: use Lazy Daisy stitch for petals (ecru) and leaves (green); use Outline stitch for stem (green); make French Knots (yellow) in center of flower. ●

MOM & ME FELTED BOOTIES **SCHEMATIC AND EMBROIDERY TEMPLATE**

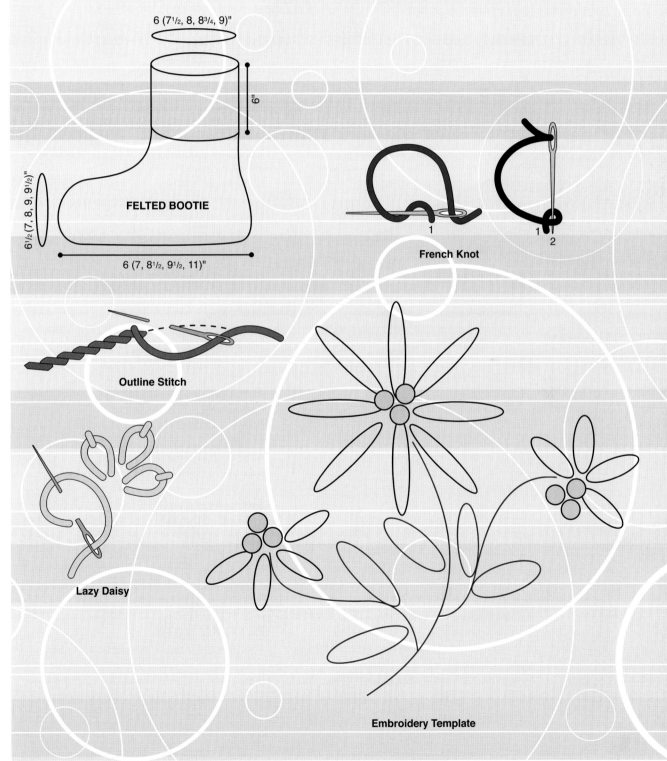

6 (7½, 8, 8¾, 9)"

9"

FELTED BOOTIE

6½ (7, 8, 9, 9½)"

6 (7, 8½, 9½, 11)"

French Knot

Outline Stitch

Lazy Daisy

Embroidery Template

MELLIFERA

DESIGN BY SARAH WILSON

You'll love wearing this whimsical design capturing the look of buzzing bees swirling around a honeycomb.

 INTERMEDIATE

SIZES
Woman's small (medium, large) Instructions are given for smallest size, with larger sizes in parentheses. When only 1 number is given, it applies to all sizes.

FINISHED MEASUREMENTS
Chest: 32¾ (35¼, 39¾) inches
Length: 23½ (24, 24½) inches

MATERIALS
Knit Picks Shine Sport Yarn (sport weight; 60% pima cotton/40% modal; 110 yds/50g per ball): 6 (8, 9) balls butter #23610
Size 4 (3.5mm) 29-inch circular needle or size needed to obtain gauge
Spare needle
Cable needle
Stitch holders
Stitch markers, 1 in CC for beg of rnd
3 yds ½-inch black grosgrain ribbon
4 (¾-inch) buttons
Sewing thread to match buttons

GAUGE
22 sts and 29 rnds = 4 inches/10cm in St st.
To save time, take time to check gauge.

SPECIAL ABBREVIATIONS
2/2 LC: Slip 2 sts to cable needle and hold to front of work; k2, k2 from cable needle.
2/2 RC: Slip 2 sts to cable needle and hold to back of work; k2, k2 from cable needle.
Place marker (pm): Place marker on needle to separate sections.

Slip marker (sm): Slip marker when you come to it.
M1L (Make 1 Left): Insert LH needle from front to back under the running thread between the last st worked and next st on LH needle; knit into the back of resulting loop.
M1R (Make 1 Right): Insert LH needle from back to front under the running thread between the last st worked and next st on LH needle. With RH needle, knit into the front of resulting loop.

PATTERN STITCH
Honeycomb and Buttonhole Pat (multiple of 8 sts + 8)
Row 1 (RS): K4, *2/2 LC, 2/2 RC; rep from * to last 4 sts, 2/2 LC.
Row 2 and all WS rows: Purl to last 4 sts, k4.
Row 3: Knit.
Row 5: K4, *2/2 RC, 2/2 LC; rep from * to last 4 sts, 2/2 RC.
Row 7 (buttonhole row): K8, yo, k2tog; knit to end.
Row 8: Rep Row 2.
    Rep Rows 1–8 for pat.

SPECIAL TECHNIQUE
3-Needle Bind-Off: With RS tog and needles parallel, using a 3rd needle, knit tog a st from the front needle with 1 from the back. *Knit tog a st from the front and back needles, and slip the first st over the 2nd to bind off. Rep from * across, then fasten off last st.

PATTERN NOTE
This sweater is made in 1 piece from the bottom up. The lower buttonband is worked back and forth, then joined for working in the round (with buttonhole band stitches overlapping buttonband stitches), then worked

to the armholes, at which point front and back are worked separately.

BODY
Honeycomb buttonband
Cast on 288 (296, 328) sts; do not join.
Row 1 (WS): K2, *p4, k4; rep from * to last 6 sts, p2, k4.
Row 2 (RS): K6, *p4, k4; rep from * to last 2 sts, k2.
Row 3: Rep Row 1.
  Work 4 reps of 8-row Honeycomb and Buttonhole pat.
Next row: Work Row 1 of Honeycomb pat to last 10 sts; place these 10 sts on spare needle.

Shape waist
Joining rnd: Holding spare needle in back, form a circle by overlapping the first 10 sts and the 10 sts on the spare needle; join first and last 10 sts as follows: [K1 from spare needle tog with st on LH needle] 10 times; dec evenly around as follows: *k2tog twice, k2, k2tog twice, k1 (2, 2); rep from * to last 4 (0, 8) sts, k2tog twice (--, k8), pm for beg of rnd—180 (194, 218) sts.

Next rnd: K24 (27, 30) left front sts, pm, k90 (97, 109) back sts, pm, k66 (70, 79) right front sts. Knit 3 rnds.
Dec rnd: *Knit to 3 sts before marker, ssk, k1, sm, k1, k2tog; rep from * once, then knit to end—176 (190, 214) sts.
  Continue in St st and rep Dec rnd [every 5 rnds] 6 times—152 (166, 190) sts.
  Knit 4 rnds.
Inc rnd: *Knit to 1 st before marker, M1R, k1, sm, k1, M1L; rep from * once, then knit to end—156 (170, 194) sts.
  Continue in St st and rep Inc rnd [every 5 rnds] 6 times—180 (194, 218) sts.
  Work even until piece measures 17 (17¼, 17½) inches.

Divide for front & back
Next rnd: K19 (20, 21) front sts, bind off 10 (14, 18) underarm sts, k80 (83, 91) back sts, bind off 10 (14, 18) underarm sts, knit to bound-off sts—80 (83, 91) sts each front and back.
  Transfer back sts to waste yarn.

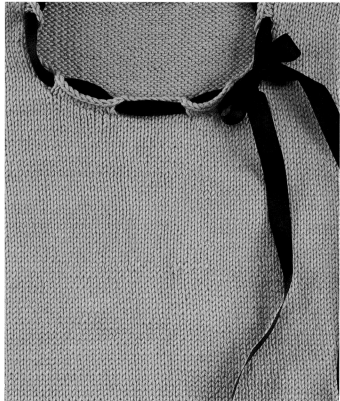

FRONT

Working in St st and beg on WS row, bind off 4 (5, 7) sts at beg of next 2 rows—72 (73, 77) sts. Work 1 row even.

Dec row (RS): K1, ssk, knit to last 3 sts, k2tog, k1—70 (71, 75) sts.

Rep Dec row [every RS row] 4 (2, 1) times, ending with a WS row—62 (67, 73) sts.

Shape neck

Next row (RS): K23, join a 2nd ball of yarn and bind off 16 (21, 27) neck sts, k23.

Working both sides at the same time with separate balls of yarn, shape neck as follows:

Row 1 (WS): Purl.

Row 2: K23; bind off 6 sts, knit to end.

Row 3: P17; bind off 6 sts, purl to end—17 sts each side.

Row 4 (dec): Knit to last 2 sts before neck, k2tog; ssk, knit to end—16 sts each side.

Row 5: Purl.

Rep last 2 rows twice more—14 sts each side.

Work even until armholes measure 6½ (6¾, 7) inches, ending with a WS row.

Cut yarn, leaving 12-inch tails.

Transfer sts to holders.

BACK

Transfer back sts to needle with WS facing and rejoin yarn.

Shape armholes as for front.

Work even until armholes measure 6½ (6¾, 7) inches, ending with a WS row.

Transfer front shoulder sts to spare needle.

With WS facing, join 14 front and back shoulder sts using 3-Needle Bind-Off; bind off 34 (39, 45) back neck sts, work 3-Needle Bind-Off across rem 14 shoulder sts.

Neck edging

Pick up and knit 100 (120, 130) sts evenly around neck edge; pm for beg of rnd and join.

Rnd 1: *K8, yo, k2tog; rep from * around.

Rnd 2: Knit.

Bind off loosely.

Sleeve edging

Pick up and knit 74 (84, 90) sts evenly around armhole edge; do not turn.

Working in the round, bind off loosely.

FINISHING

Weave in all ends. Block to finished measurements.

Sew buttons to underlapped buttonband to match buttonholes.

Weave ribbon through eyelet holes at neckline, beg and ending at left front.

Tie ribbon in a bow, leaving tails to hang down front of sweater. ●

MELLIFERA **SCHEMATIC AND CHART**

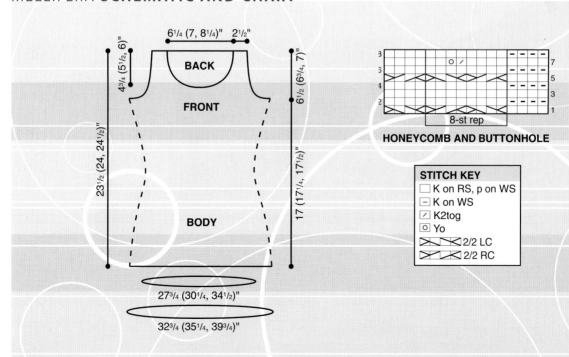

HONEYCOMB AND BUTTONHOLE

STITCH KEY
☐ K on RS, p on WS
─ K on WS
╱ K2tog
○ Yo
2/2 LC
2/2 RC

SIMPLE**summer**SWEATER

DESIGN BY ANDRA KNIGHT-BOWMAN

Perfectly understated. This casual design is the right choice for any occasion.

 EASY

SIZES
Woman's small (medium, large, extra-large, 2X-large) Instructions are given for smallest size, with larger sizes in parentheses. When only 1 number is given, it applies to all sizes.

FINISHED MEASUREMENTS
Chest: 36 (40, 44, 48, 52) inches
Length: 20 (21, 22, 23, 24½) inches

MATERIALS
Artyarns Ultramerino 6 (DK weight; 100% merino wool; 274 yds/100g per hank): 3 (4, 4, 5, 5) hanks green/yellow #UM6-133
Size 7 (4.5mm) 16- and 32-inch circular needles or size needed to obtain gauge
Stitch markers, 1 in CC for beg of rnd

3 LIGHT

GAUGE
20 sts and 32 rnds = 4 inches/10cm in St st.
To save time, take time to check gauge.

SPECIAL ABBREVIATION
Make 1 (M1): Insert LH needle from front to back under the running thread between the last st worked and next st on RH needle; knit into the back of resulting loop.

SPECIAL TECHNIQUE
3-Needle Bind-Off: With RS tog and needles parallel, using a 3rd needle, knit tog a st from the front needle with 1 from the back. *Knit tog a st from the front and back needles, and slip the first st over the 2nd to bind off. Rep from * across, then fasten off last st.

PATTERN NOTES
This shell is worked from the bottom up; first lower garter stitch borders are worked, then joined and body is knit in the round to underarms; front and back are worked separately from armhole to shoulder. A wide garter stitch collar is worked after garment is complete.

Slip first stitch of all rows purlwise with yarn in front; bring yarn to back and continue to work row.

BOTTOM BORDERS
Cast on 90 (100, 110, 120, 130) sts.
Rows 1–10: Sl 1, knit to end.
Row 11 (WS): Sl 1, k5, purl to last 6 sts, knit to end.
Row 2 (RS): Sl 1, knit to end.
Rep [Rows 1 and 2] 6 times more; cut yarn and leave sts on needle.
Rep for 2nd border; after last row, do not turn and do not cut yarn.

BODY
Rnd 1: Place marker for beg of rnd and knit across first set of border sts, place marker for side and knit across 2nd set of border sts.
Work even in St st for 12½ (13, 13½, 14, 15) inches.

Divide for Back and Front
Next row: Sl 1, k5, ssk, knit to 8 sts before side marker, k2tog, k6, turn; transfer rem sts to waste yarn for front—88 (98, 108, 118, 128) back sts.

BACK
Row 1 (WS): Sl 1, k5, purl to last 6 sts, k6.
Row 2 (RS): Sl 1, k5, ssk, knit to last 8 sts, k2tog, k6—86 (96, 106, 116, 126) sts.
Rep [last 2 rows] 11 (11, 11, 12, 16) more times—64 (74, 84, 92, 94) sts.

Work even until armhole measures 7½ (8, 8½, 9, 9½) inches.

Place first 17 (20, 23, 26, 26) shoulder sts, 30 (34, 38, 40, 42) back neck sts, and last 17 (20, 23, 26, 26) shoulder sts on separate lengths of waste yarn.

FRONT

Work as for back until armholes measure 5½ (6, 6½, 7, 7½) inches, ending with a WS row.

Shape Neck

Row 1 (RS): Sl 1, k21 (24, 27, 30, 30), place center 20 (24, 28, 30, 32) sts on waste yarn, attach new yarn, k22 (25, 28, 31, 31).

Row 2 (dec): Work to 3 sts before neck edge, ssp, p1; p1, p2tog, work to end—21 (24, 27, 30, 30) sts each side.

Row 3 (dec): Work to 3 sts before neck edge, k2tog, k1; k1, ssk, work to end—20 (23, 26, 29, 29) sts each side.

Continue to dec at each neck edge [every row] 3 (3, 3, 2, 2) more times—17 (20, 23, 26, 26) sts each side.

Work even until armhole measures 7½ (8, 8½, 9, 9½) inches.

ASSEMBLY

Transfer left back shoulder sts to needle. Join shoulder using 3-Needle Bind-Off.

Rep for right shoulder.

Weave in ends and block to finished measurements.

COLLAR

With RS facing and 16-inch needle, beg at shoulder, pick up and knit 77 (84, 91, 98, 105) sts around neck, including sts from back neck waste yarn; place marker for beg of rnd and join.

Beg and end with a purl rnd, work 2 inches in garter st.

Inc rnd: *K7, M1; rep from * around—88 (96, 104, 112, 120) sts.

Continue in garter st for 1 inch, ending with a purl rnd.

Inc rnd: *K8, M1; rep from * around—99 (108, 117, 126, 135) sts.

Work even in garter st for 1 inch.

Inc rnd: *K9, M1; rep from * around—110 (120, 130, 137, 150) sts.

Work even in garter st for 1 inch.

Bind off loosely. ●

SIMPLE SUMMER SWEATER **SCHEMATIC**

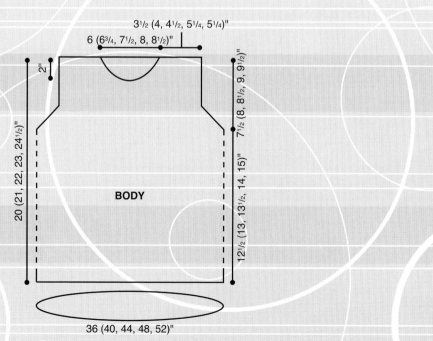

3½ (4, 4½, 5¼, 5¼)"

6 (6¾, 7½, 8, 8½)"

2"

20 (21, 22, 23, 24½)"

BODY

7½ (8, 8½, 9, 9½)"

12½ (13, 13½, 14, 15)"

36 (40, 44, 48, 52)"

FLEUR**jumper**

DESIGN BY AMY MARSHALL

If you love intarsia, you'll find this irresistible jumper a joy to create.

▰▰▰▱ INTERMEDIATE

SIZES
Infant's 3–6 (6–12, 12–18, 18–24) months
Instructions are given for smallest size, with larger sizes in parentheses. When only 1 number is given, it applies to all sizes.

FINISHED MEASUREMENTS
Chest: 20¾ (22½, 24, 25½) inches
Length: 14¾ (16, 17¾, 19½) inches

MATERIALS
Filatura Di Crosa Zara (DK weight; 100% merino wool; 137 yds/50g per ball): 2 balls light yellow #1651 (MC); 1 ball each true blue #1754 (A), bright light blue #1472 (B), light blue #1462 (C), kelly green #1727 (D)
Size 6 (4mm) double-point (set of 4), 16- and 29-inch circular needles or size needed to obtain gauge
Size F/5 (3.75mm) crochet hook
Stitch markers, 1 in CC for beg of rnd
Bobbins (optional)

3 LIGHT

GAUGE
20 sts and 28 rnds = 4 inches/10cm in St st.
To save time, take time to check gauge.

SPECIAL ABBREVIATIONS
Place marker (pm): Place a marker on needle to separate sections.
Slip marker (sm): Slip marker when you come to it.
Make 1 (M1): Insert LH needle from front to back under the running thread between the last st worked and next st on RH needle; knit into the back of resulting loop.

SPECIAL TECHNIQUE
3-Needle Bind-Off: With RS tog and needles parallel, using a 3rd needle, knit tog a st from the front needle with 1 from the back. *Knit tog a st from the front and back needles, and slip the first st over the 2nd to bind off. Rep from * across, then fasten off last st.

PATTERN STITCHES
Stripe sequence
*Knit 2 rnds A, 2 rnds B, 2 rnds C; rep from * as necessary.
Flower pat (40-st panel)
See Chart.

PATTERN NOTES
This jumper is worked in the round from the bottom to the armholes, at which point front and back are separated and worked back and forth. The short sleeves begin in the round; the cap is worked back and forth.

Minimize the color jog between stripes as follows: before beginning 2nd round of a new color, pick up the stitch in the row below the first stitch of the round (it will be the old color)

and place it on the left needle; knit it together with the first stitch of the round.

When working flower pattern, use intarsia technique, page 170, with a separate length of yarn for each colored section; bring new color up from under old color to interlock them. Put lengths of yarn on bobbins, if desired.

BODY

With longer circular needle and D, cast on 136 (144, 152, 160) sts; pm for beg of rnd and join, taking care not to twist sts.

Work in K2, P2 Rib for 1 inch.

Beg Stripe sequence

Next rnd: Change to A and St st; *k23 (24, 25, 26), pm, k22 (24, 26, 28), pm, k23 (24, 25, 26); rep from * once more.

Work 1 more rnd A.

Continue with Stripe sequence until piece measures 2¼ (2¼, 2¾, 3) inches.

Dec rnd: Maintaining Stripe sequence, *k2, ssk, work to marker, sm; k2, ssk, [work to 4 sts before next marker, k2tog, k2, sm] twice; rep from * once more—128 (136, 144, 152) sts.

Maintain Stripe sequence and rep Dec rnd [every 14 (16, 18, 20) rnds] 3 times—104 (112, 120, 128) sts.

Change to MC and work even in St st until piece measures 10 (11, 12½, 14) inches.

Place last 52 (56, 60, 64) sts on waste yarn for back.

FRONT

Row 1 (RS): Bind off 2 sts, knit to end, removing markers—50 (54, 58, 62) sts.

Row 2: Bind off 2 sts, p4 (6, 8, 10) [including st from bind off], pm, purl to 4 (6, 8, 10) sts, pm, purl to end—48 (52, 56, 60) sts.

Dec row (RS): Begin working Flower chart between markers and at the same time, dec as follows: k2, ssk, work to last 4 sts, k2tog, k2—46 (50, 54, 58) sts.

Work Dec row [every RS row] 2 (2, 2, 3) times—44 (48, 50, 52) sts.

Work even until armhole measures 2¾ (3, 3, 3¼) inches, ending with a WS row.

Note: *When chart is complete, continue in St st with MC.*

Front neck

Next row (RS): Work 15 (16, 17, 18) sts; join 2nd ball of yarn and bind off center 14 (16, 16, 16) sts, work to end of row.

Working both sides at once with separate balls of yarn, purl 1 row.

Dec row (RS): Knit to last 4 sts before neck, k2tog, k2; k2, ssk, knit to end—14 (15, 16, 17) sts each side.

Rep Dec row [every RS row] 4 times—10 (11, 12, 13) sts.

Work even until armhole measures 4¾ (5, 5¼, 5½) inches.

Put rem sts on waste yarn.

BACK

Transfer back sts to needle with RS facing; join yarn.

Bind off 2 sts at beg of next 2 rows—48 (52, 56, 60) sts.

Dec row (RS): K2, ssk, work to last 4 sts, k2tog, k2—46 (50, 54, 58) sts.

Rep Dec row [every RS row] 2 (2, 2, 3) times—44 (48, 50, 52) sts.

Work even in St st until armhole measures 4 (4¼, 4½, 4¾) inches, ending with a WS row.

Back neck

Next row (RS): Work 14 (15, 16, 17) sts, join 2nd ball of yarn and bind off center 16 (18, 18, 18) sts, work to end of row.

Work both sides at once with separate balls of yarn.

Dec row (WS): Purl to 4 sts before neck, p2tog, p2; p2, ssp, purl to end—13 (14, 15, 16) sts each side.

Dec row (RS): Knit to 4 sts before neck, ssk, k2; k2, k2tog, knit to end—12 (13, 14, 15) sts each side.

Rep last 2 rows once more—10 (11, 12, 13) sts each side.

Work even until armhole measures 4¾ (5, 5¼, 5½) inches.

Put rem sts on waste yarn.

SLEEVES

With dpns and MC, cast on 36 (36, 40, 40) sts; pm for beg of rnd and join, taking care not to twist sts.

Work 3 rnds in K2, P2 Rib.

Inc rnd: K2, M1, knit to last 2 sts, M1, k2—38 (40, 42, 42) sts.

Rep Inc rnd [every other rnd] 1 (2, 1, 2) more time(s)—40 (42, 44, 46) sts.

Work even until piece measures 1 inch.

Shape cap

Begin working back and forth.

Bind off 2 sts at the beg of the next 2 rows—36 (38, 40, 42) sts.

Dec row (RS): K2, ssk, knit to last 4 sts, k2tog, k2—34 (36, 38, 40) sts.

Rep Dec row [every RS row] 9 (10, 11, 12) times then [every row] 3 times—10 sts.

Bind off.

FINISHING

Join shoulder seams with 3-Needle Bind-Off.

Weave in ends; block pieces to finished measurements.

NECKBAND

With RS facing, using shorter needle and MC, pick up and knit 64 (68, 72, 72) sts evenly around neck opening; pm for beg of rnd and join.

Work K2, P2 Rib for ½ inch.

Bind off loosely in rib.

Sew sleeves to body.

Weave in rem ends.

With crochet hook and D, embroider stems and leaves using chain stitch (see photo). ●

FLEUR JUMPER **SCHEMATICS AND CHART**

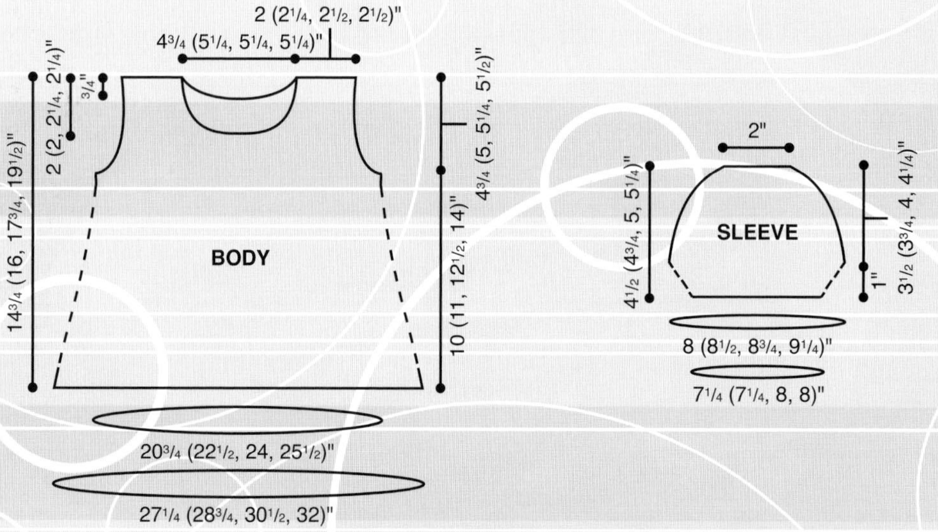

2 (2¼, 2½, 2½)"
4¾ (5¼, 5¼, 5¼)"
¾"
2 (2, 2¼, 2¼)"
14¾ (16, 17¾, 19½)"
BODY
4¾ (5, 5¼, 5½)"
10 (11, 12½, 14)"
20¾ (22½, 24, 25½)"
27¼ (28¾, 30½, 32)"
2"
SLEEVE
4½ (4¾, 5, 5¼)"
1"
3½ (3¾, 4, 4¼)"
8 (8½, 8¾, 9¼)"
7¼ (7¼, 8, 8)"

COLOR KEY
- Light yellow (MC)
- True blue (A)
- Bright light blue (B)
- Kelly green (D)

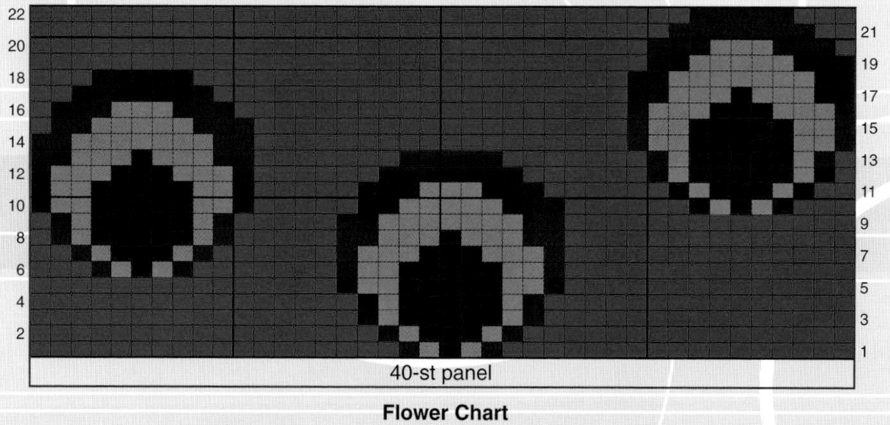

22
20
18
16
14
12
10
8
6
4
2
21
19
17
15
13
11
9
7
5
3
1
40-st panel

Flower Chart

CLEMENTINE**felted**CARRYALL

DESIGN BY ANN SQUIRE

This sassy felted sack will hold your knitting projects in style.

▬▬▬▭ INTERMEDIATE

FINISHED MEASUREMENTS
Before Felting:
Circumference: 50 inches
Height: 15 inches
After Felting:
Circumference: 36 inches
Height: 10 inches

MATERIALS
Brown Sheep Lamb's Pride Bulky (bulky weight; 85% wool/15% mohair; 125 yds/113g per skein): 3 skeins autumn harvest #M22 (A), 1 skein chianti #M28 (B), 1 skein rust #M97 (C)
Brown Sheep Lamb's Pride Worsted (worsted weight; 85% wool/15% mohair; 190 yds/113g per skein): 1 skein amethyst #M62 (D)

Crystal Palace Fizz (eyelash yarn; 100% polyester; 120 yds/50g per ball): 1 ball tangerine #7301 (E)
Crystal Palace Squiggle (eyelash yarn; 100% polyester; 110 yds/50g per ball): 1 ball mango orange #2268 (F)
Size 6 (4mm) needles
Size 10½ (6.5mm) double-point needles (set of 4)
Size 13 (9mm) double-point (set of 5) and 30-inch circular needles or size needed to obtain gauge
Stitch marker
Stitch holder (optional)
Sewing thread and needle
Pin back or large safety pin

PRE-FELT GAUGE
10 sts and 14 rnds = 4 inches/10cm in St st on size 13 needles with A, B or C.
Exact gauge is not critical; make sure your sts are loose and airy.

SPECIAL ABBREVIATION
Increase 1 (inc1): Knit in front and back of st.

SPECIAL TECHNIQUES
I-Cord Bind-Off: At beg of rnd, cast on 5 sts. *K4, k2tog-tbl, do not turn. Slip 5 sts back to LH needle and rep from * around until all sts are bound off. Bind off I-cord sts.
I-Cord: Cast on 6 sts. *K6, do not turn, slip sts back to LH needle; rep from * until cord is desired length. Bind off.

PATTERN NOTES

Change to circular needle when there are enough stitches to do so.

The base is worked in garter stitch (purl 1 round, knit 1 round); the sides are worked in stockinette stitch (knit all rounds).

At each color change, cut old yarn and join new yarn. To avoid color jog, slip first stitch of second round of each new color; knit all other rounds as usual.

BASE

With size 13 dpns and A, cast on 8 sts. Distribute sts evenly on 4 dpns; pm for beg of rnd and join, taking care not to twist sts.

Rnd 1: Work in garter st, beg with a purl rnd.

Next rnd (inc): Maintaining garter st, inc1 in each st around—16 sts.

Work 5 rnds even in garter st as established. Rep [last 6 rnds] twice more—64 sts.

Next rnd (inc): *K1, inc1; rep from * around—96 sts.

Work 5 rnds even in garter st.

Next rnd (inc): *K2, inc 1; rep from * around—128 sts.

Work 4 rnds even in garter st.

Purl 3 rnds.

SIDES

Knit 5 rnds A.

Knit 2 rnds B, remembering to slip first st of 2nd rnd to avoid color jog (see Pattern Notes).

Knit 6 rnds C.

Knit 2 rnds B.

Knit 6 rnds A.

Knit 3 rnds C.

Knit 4 rnds B.

Knit 3 rnds C.

Knit 6 rnds A.

Knit 4 rnds B.

Knit 2 rnds C.

Knit 4 rnds B.

Knit 4 rnds A.

Next rnd (dec): With A, *k14, k2tog; rep from * around—120 sts.

Work I-cord bind-off around, then sew ends of I-cord tog.

Weave in ends.

HANDLES
Make 2

With size 13 dpns and A, cast on 6 sts.

Work I-cord for 23 inches.

Bind off.

With tapestry needle and A, sew handles firmly to inside edge of bag.

FLOWER
Center

With size 10½ dpns and D, cast on 5 sts. Distribute sts on 3 dpns; place marker for beg of rnd, and join, taking care not to twist sts.

Rnd 1: Knit.

Rnd 2: Inc1 in each st around—10 sts.

Rnds 3 and 4: Knit.

Rnd 5: Inc1 in each st around—20 sts.

Rnd 6: Knit.

Slip first 16 sts onto waste yarn or holder.

Petals
Make 5

Work rem 4 sts back and forth on 2 dpns to form first petal.

Row 1: Knit.

Row 2: [Inc1, k1] twice—6 sts.

Row 3: Knit.

Row 4: Inc1, k3, inc1, k1—8 sts.

Row 5: Knit.

Row 6: Inc1, k5, inc1, k1—10 sts.

Rows 7–12: Knit.

Row 13: K1, ssk, k4, k2tog, k1—8 sts.

Row 14: Knit.

Row 15: K1, ssk, k2, k2tog, k1—6 sts.

Row 16: Knit.

Row 17: K1, ssk, k2tog, k1—4 sts.

Row 18: K2tog twice—2 sts.

Cut yarn; pull tail through rem 2 sts to fasten off.

To beg next petal, slip 4 sts from waste yarn onto dpn and rep Rows 1–18.

Continue until all 5 petals are complete.

Weave in ends.

FELTING

Felt bag and flower separately following basic felting instructions on page 171 until finished measurements are obtained or pieces are desired size.

Block bag to desired shape (stuff bag with towels or crumpled plastic bags) and let dry completely.

Pull flower into shape and dry flat.

Flower Center

With size 6 needles and 1 strand each of E and F held tog, cast on 2 sts, leaving a 5-inch tail.

Row 1: Inc1 in each st—4 sts.
Row 2: Knit.
Row 3: Inc1 in each st—8 sts.
Row 4: Knit.
Row 5: K2tog across—4 sts.
Row 6: K2tog across—2 sts.

Cut yarn, leaving a 5-inch tail; pull tail through rem 2 sts to fasten off.

Tie yarn tails tog, pulling tight to give flower center a rounded shape; cut tails.

After flower has been felted, use needle and thread to attach flower center to body of flower.

Sew pin back or safety pin to back of flower and pin to bag where desired. ●

TAKE**itfromthe top-down**

Now that you're a circular knitting diva, we think you're ready to move into some new territory. Try your hand at the Aztec Top, or some simple standbys, such as the Mock Mobius Cowl or the Shell Tote.

SPECIAL ways OF working

Now that you have a good grounding in circular knitting, working from the top-down has some great advantages. Since you begin from the neck opening, your most crucial shaping sections, such as armholes and bust, are worked first, long before the waist shaping. This saves you from the possible nightmare of knitting flat pieces and seaming them together, only to realize that your waist shaping was incorrect! With the top-down method, your shaping elements have been determined, allowing some "creative license" to lengthen your sweater or make it slightly shorter, if preferred.

Engineered Elements

As stressed in previous chapters, the schematic is always positioned the way the garment will be worked, with top-down projects, you will notice that the schematic is positioned upside down, with the neck as the cast-on round.

Shown in the illustration above, after casting on for the back neck, you will work the raglan shaping for the fronts, back and sleeves at the same time that you are shaping the V-neck; since the V-neck is "open", you will be working back and forth. After the V-neck shaping is complete, you will join the two ends of the piece at the front neck and continue by working in the round. When the raglan shaping is done, you will bind off the sleeve stitches, and then continue working the body, shaping the waist before binding off.

Shaping Elements

Circular knitting takes on a 3-dimensional form, unlike static flat, back-and-forth knitting. There are many ways to work a circular design because of its "sculptural" aspects. For example, fitted sections of the waist and bust can be worked in a simpler way than one would do with a project knitted flat. With top-down knitting, you can literally try the piece on while you work.

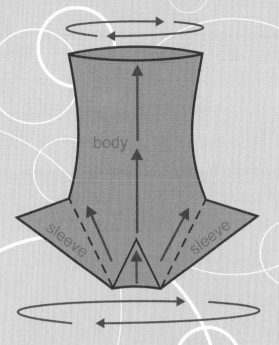

Here are some common shapes found in circular knitting that can "molded" into different forms:

- Straight, Unshaped Tubes: Can become neck warmers, tote bags, fingerless gloves or the body of a pullover.
- Shaped Tubes: Become sleeves, hats and waist-shaping sections on the body of a pullover.
- Cones: Usually a very shallow cone can become the yoke of a sweater, worked with proportionally spaced decrease rounds.
- Domes: Commonly found in hats, where shaping sections are evenly spaced, until most of the stitches are severely decreased to the top.

HOW TO To make a neater join, cast on one more stitch than called for in your pattern onto your circular needle, or double-point needles, and then slip the first stitch from the left-hand needle onto the right-hand needle. Lift the next stitch on the right-hand needle and place it over the slipped stitch. This creates a smooth cast-on edge.

AZTEC**top**

DESIGN BY JEAN CLEMENT

Based on the "pretzel" sweater concept, this top is flattering and fun to knit. Wear it on its own or as a vest on a cool crisp day.

■■■□ INTERMEDIATE

SIZES
Woman's small (medium, large, extra-large, 2X-large, 3X-large) Instructions are given for smallest size, with larger sizes in parentheses. If only 1 number is given, it applies to all sizes.

FINISHED MEASUREMENTS
Chest: 34¾, (39¾, 43½, 47¾, 51½, 55) inches
Length: 20½ (21¼, 23¾, 25¼, 26½, 27¼) inches

MATERIALS
Crystal Palace Yarns Panda Silk (fingering weight; 52% bamboo/ 43% superwash merino wool/ 5% combed silk; 204 yds/50g per ball): 6 (7, 8, 9, 9, 10) balls plum tones #4006

1 SUPER FINE

Size 2.5 (3mm) 16- and 20-inch circular needles
Size 5 (3.75mm) 24- and 36-inch circular needles or size needed to obtain gauge
Stitch markers, 1 in CC for beg of rnd
Several yards of scrap yarn for holding stitches

GAUGE
26 sts and 55 rnds = 4 inches/10cm in Body pat with larger needles.
To save time, take time to check gauge.

SPECIAL ABBREVIATIONS
Place marker (pm): Place a marker on the needle.
Slip marker (sm): Slip the marker.
Make 1 (M1): Insert LH needle from front to back under the running thread between the last st worked and next st on RH needle; knit into the back of resulting loop.

SPECIAL TECHNIQUE
3-Needle Bind-Off
With RS tog and needles parallel, using a 3rd needle, knit tog a st from the front needle with 1 from the back. *Knit tog a st from the front and back needles, and slip the first st over the 2nd to bind off. Rep from * across, then fasten off last st.

PATTERN STITCH
Body Pattern for Gauge (odd number of sts)
   Cast on odd number of sts and work in rounds.
Rnds 1 and 2: *K1, sl 1; rep from * around.
Rnd 3: Knit around.
Rnd 4: Purl around.
Rnds 5 and 6: Knit around.
Rnds 7 and 8: Purl around.
   Rep Rnds 1–8 for gauge pat.

PATTERN NOTES
This sweater is worked in the round as a large rectangle, beginning in the center at the neck which is worn vertically (see diagram). When rectangle is finished, side seams are joined using 3-Needle Bind-Off.

   The body rectangle is worked in following order: right side, back, left side, front.

   Front and back sections are increased every other round; side sections are increased every 4th round.

   The fiber content of the yarn used has quite a bit of drape and will cause the project to stretch lengthwise. Wet-block to measurements given on the schematic and lay flat to dry; do not move the sweater until it is thoroughly dry.

   Work gauge swatch in the round using pattern stitch given above.

92   CIRCULAR KNITTING REDEFINED

Change to longer circular needle when stitches no longer fit comfortably on working needle.

TOP

Beg at neckline with smaller 16-inch circular needle, cast on 135 (135, 143, 153, 161, 161) sts, pm, cast on 135 (135, 143, 153, 161, 161) sts; place marker for beg of rnd and join, taking care not to twist sts—270 (270, 286, 306, 322, 322) sts.

Rnds 1 and 2: [*K1, p1; rep from * to st before marker, k1] twice.

BORDER

Rnd 1: [K1, M1, k1, *sl 1, k1; rep from * to 1 st before marker, M1, k1, sm] twice—4 incs made.

Rnd 2 and all even-number rnds: Knit.

Rnd 3: [K1, M1, k2, *sl 1 wyif, k1; rep from * to 2 sts before marker, k1, M1, k1, sm] twice—4 incs made.

Rnd 5: [K1, M1, k2, *sl 1, k1; rep from * to 2 sts before marker, k1, M1, k1, sm] twice—4 incs made.

Rnd 7: [K1, M1, k1, *sl 1 wyif, k1; rep from * to 1 st before marker, M1, k1, sm] twice—4 incs made.

Rnd 8: Knit.

Rep Rnds 1–8 of Border 1 (1, 2, 2, 2, 2) more time(s)—302 (302, 334, 354, 370, 370) sts.

BODY

Change to larger 36-inch circular needle.

Rnd 1 (set-up rnd): Right side: k1, M1, purl to 1 st before marker, M1, k1, sm; back: M1, pm; left side: k1, M1, purl to 1 st before marker, M1, k1, pm; front: M1—308 (308, 340, 360, 376, 376) sts with 153 (153, 169, 179, 187, 187) sts each right/left sides and 1 st each front/back.

Rnd 2: [K1, purl to 1 st before marker, k1, sm; p1] twice.

Rnd 3: [K1, M1, k1, *sl 1, k1; rep from * to 1 st before marker, M1, k1, sm; M1, k1, M1, sm] twice—8 incs made, 2 each side, front and back.

Rnd 4: [K3, *sl 1; rep from * to 2 sts before marker, k2, sm, k3] twice.

Rnd 5: [Knit to marker, sm; M1, knit to marker, M1, sm] twice—4 incs made, 2 each front and back.

Rnd 6: [K1, purl to 1 st before marker, k1, sm, purl to marker, sm] twice.

Rnd 7: [K1, M1, knit to 1 st before marker, M1, k1, sm; M1, knit to marker, M1, sm] twice—8 incs made, 2 each side, front and back.

Rnd 8: Knit around.

Rnd 9: [K1, purl to 1 st before marker, k1, sm;

M1, purl to marker, M1, sm] twice—4 incs made, 2 each front and back.

Rnd 10: [K1, purl to 1 st before marker, k1, sm; purl to marker, sm] twice.

Rnd 11: [K1, M1, k1, *sl 1, k1; rep from * to 1 st before marker, M1, k1, sm; M1, k1, *sl 1, k1; rep from * to marker, M1, sm] twice—8 incs made, 2 each side, front and back.

Rnd 12: [K3, *sl 1, k1; rep from * to 2 sts before marker, k2, sm; k2, *sl 1, k1; rep from * to 1 st before marker, k1, sm] twice.

Rep [Rnds 5–12] 12 (14, 15, 17, 19, 20) times, then work Rnds 5–8 (5–8, 5–10, 5–10, 5–6, 5–10) once more—640 (688, 748, 816, 868, 904) sts with 209 (217, 235, 255, 269, 275) sts each right/left sides and 111 (127, 139, 153, 165, 177) sts each front/back.

Next rnd (sizes S and M only): Purl around.

Cut yarn.

Transfer right and left side sts to separate pieces of scrap yarn; transfer front and back sts tog onto 1 piece of scrap yarn, including the 4 knit edge sts from side sections—207 (215, 233, 253, 267, 273) each side sts and 226 (258, 282, 310, 334, 358) bottom (front/back) sts.

Join sides

Transfer one set of side sts to larger needle.

With RS tog and both ends of needle facing the same direction, join first and last 52 (53, 57, 62, 66, 67) side sts (lower edge) using 3-Needle

Bind-Off—center 103 (109, 119, 129, 135, 139) sts rem.

ARMHOLE BORDERS
Transfer rem sts to smaller 16-inch needle.
Set-up rnd: Purl around, M1, pm, join to work in rnd—104 (110, 120, 130, 136, 140) sts.
Rnd 1: *K1, sl 1; rep from * around.
Rnd 2 and all even-number rnds: Knit around.
Rnd 3: *K1, *sl 1 wyif; rep from * around.
Rnd 5: *Sl 1, k1; rep from * around.
Rnd 7: *Sl 1 wyif, k1; rep from * around.
Rnd 8: Knit around.
Rep [Rnds 1–8] 1 (1, 1, 2, 2, 2) time(s).
Next 2 rnds: *K1, p1; rep from * around.
   Bind off in rib.
   Rep seam joining and armhole border for 2nd side.

LOWER BORDER
Transfer bottom sts to larger needle.
   With RS of back facing, join yarn and purl across back sts, pick up and purl 2 sts at side seam, purl across front sts, pick up and purl 2 sts at side seam, pm—230 (262, 286, 314, 338, 362) sts.
   Rep [8-rnd armhole border pat] 2 (2, 2, 3, 3, 3) times.
   Change to smaller needle.
Next 2 rnds: *K1, p1; rep from * around.
   Bind off loosely in rib, using larger needle as working needle.

FINISHING
Weave in all ends.
   Block to finished measurements as shown on schematic. ●

AZTEC TOP **SCHEMATIC AND DIAGRAM**

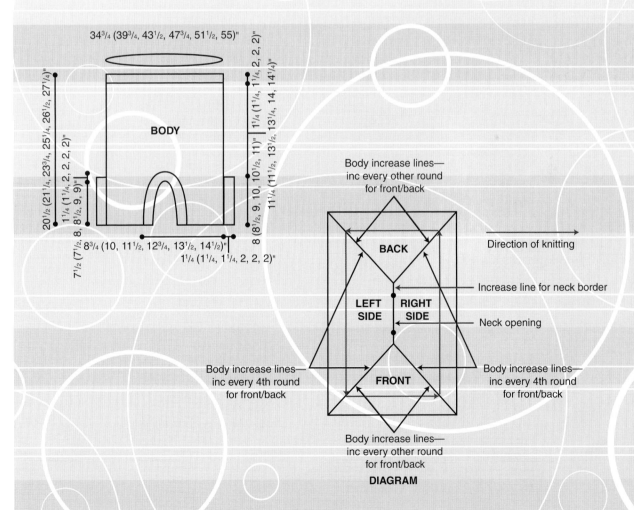

STRUCTURED**rib**PULLOVER

DESIGN BY FAINA GOBERSTEIN

With tailored details, this fitted pullover is the perfect new classic for your wardrobe.

 **INTERMEDIATE**

SIZES
Woman's small (medium, large, extra-large) Instructions are given for smallest size, with larger sizes in parentheses. When only 1 number is given, it applies to all sizes.

FINISHED MEASUREMENTS
Chest: 33½ (36¼, 40, 43¾) inches
Length: 27 (29, 29½, 30½) inches

MATERIALS
RYC Silk Wool DK (DK weight; 50% merino wool/50% silk; 109 yds/ 50g per ball): 10 (12, 14, 16) balls limewash #00301
Size 4 (3.5mm) 24-inch circular needle
Size 6 (4mm) double-point (set of 4 or 5), 16- and 29-inch circular needles or size needed to obtain gauge
Size 7 (4.5mm) 24-inch circular needle
Size G/6 (4mm) crochet hook
Stitch markers, 1 in CC for beg of rnd

3 LIGHT

GAUGE
25 sts and 29 rnds = 4 inches/10cm in Flowery Rib with size 6 needle.
24 sts and 30 rows = 4 inches/10cm in Seed Stitch using size 6 needle.
To save time, take time to check gauge.

SPECIAL ABBREVIATIONS
Place marker (pm): Place a marker on needle to separate sections.
Slip marker (sm): Slip marker when you come to it.
Edge st: At beg of row: sl 1 pwise wyif; at end of row: k1-tbl.
Make 1 Left Purlwise (M1L-P): Insert LH needle from front to back under the running thread between the last st worked and next st on LH needle; purl into the back of resulting loop.
Make 1 Right Purlwise (M1R-P): Insert LH needle from back to front under the running thread between the last st worked and next st on LH needle. With RH needle, purl into the front of resulting loop.
Make 1 Left (M1L): Insert LH needle from front to back under the running thread between the last st worked and next st on LH needle; knit into the back of resulting loop.
Make 1 Right (M1R): Insert LH needle from back to front under the running thread between the last st worked and next st on LH needle. With RH needle, knit into the front of resulting loop.

STITCH PATTERNS
Flowery Rib (back and forth) (multiple of 8 sts)
Rows 1 and 3 (RS): *K1, p3; rep from * to end.
Rows 2 and 4: *K3, p1; rep from * to end.
Row 5: *K1, p2, k1, p1, k1, p2; rep from * to end.
Row 6: *K2, p1, k1, p1, k2, p1; rep from * to end.
Row 7: *K1, p1; rep from * to end.
Row 8: *P1, k1; rep from * to end.
Rows 9 and 10: Rep Rows 5 and 6.
Rep Rows 1–10 for pat.

Flowery Rib (in the round) (multiple of 8 sts)
Rnds 1–4: *K1, p3; rep from * around.
Rnds 5 and 6: *K1, p2, k1, p1, k1, p2; rep from * around.
Rnds 7 and 8: *K1, p1; rep from * around.
Rnds 9 and 10: Rep Rnds 5 and 6.
Rep Rnds 1–10 for pat.

Seed Stitch
Rnd/Row 1: *P1, k1; rep from *, ending p1 if an odd number of sts.
Pat rnd/row: Knit the purl sts and purl the knit sts.
Rep Pat rnd for pat.

SPECIAL TECHNIQUES

Provisional Cast-On: With crochet hook and waste yarn, make a chain several sts longer than desired cast on. With knitting needle and project yarn, pick up indicated number of sts in the "bumps" on back of chain. When indicated in pat, "unzip" the crochet chain and place live sts on needle.

3-Needle Bind-Off: With RS tog and needles parallel, using a 3rd needle, knit tog a st from the front needle with one from the back. *Knit tog a st from the front and back needles, and slip the first st over the 2nd to bind off. Rep from * across, then fasten off last st.

PATTERN NOTES

This square-necked raglan pullover is worked in one piece from the top down. The front neck is bordered with seed stitch. When yoke is complete, the body and sleeves are separated and worked individually in the round.

The charts give the first 14 rows of the raglan increase pattern; after completing charts, continue to work raglan increases, working new stitches into established Flowery Rib pattern as they accumulate and maintaining established seed stitch at front edges.

When working sleeves, change to double-point needles when stitches no longer fit comfortably on circular needle.

YOKE

With longer size 6 circular needle, cast on 6 (7, 9, 10) right front sts, pm; 3 raglan sts, pm; 9 (11, 15, 17) sleeve sts, pm; 3 raglan sts, pm; 25 (27, 31, 33) back sts, pm; 3 raglan sts, pm; 9 (11, 15, 17) sleeve sts, pm; 3 raglan sts, pm; 6 (7, 9, 10) left front sts; do not join—67 (75, 91, 99) sts.

Raglan & Neck Shaping

Set-up row (WS): Edge st, [p1, k1] 2 (3, 3, 3) times, p1 (0, 0, 0), k0 (0, 2, 2), p0 (0, 0,1), M1R-P; sm, p3, sm; M1L-P, k0 (1, 3, 0), [p1, k3] 2 (2, 2, 4) times, p1, k0 (1, 3, 0), M1R-P; sm, p3, sm; M1L-P, k0 (1, 3, 0), [p1, k3] 6 (6, 7, 8) times, p1 (1, 0, 1), k0 (1, 0, 0), M1R-P; sm, p3, sm; M1L-P, k0 (1, 3, 0), [p1, k3] 2 (2, 2, 4) times, p1, k0 (1, 3, 0), M1R-P; sm, p3, sm; M1L-P, p0 (0, 0,1), k0 (1, 3, 3), p1, [k1, p1] twice, edge st—75 (83, 99, 107) sts.

Row 1 (RS): Edge st, [p1, k1] twice, k1, p1 (2, 3, 3), k0 (0, 1, 1), p0 (0, 0,1); sm, k1, p1, k1, sm; p1 (2, 0, 1), [k1, p3] 2 (2, 4, 4) times, k1, p1 (2, 0, 1); sm, k1, p1, k1, sm; p1 (2, 0, 1), [k1, p3] 6 (6, 8, 8) times,

k1, p1 (2, 0, 1); sm, k1, p1, k1, sm; p1 (2, 0, 1), [k1, p3] 2 (2, 4, 4) times, k1, p1 (2, 0, 1); sm, k1, p1, k1, sm; p0 (0, 0, 1), k0 (0, 1, 1), p1 (2, 3, 3), k1, [k1, p1] twice, edge st.

Row 2 (inc): Edge st, [p1, k1] 3 times, k0 (1, 2, 2), p0 (0, 1, 1), k0 (0, 0, 1), M1R-P; sm, p3, sm; M1L-P, k1 (2, 0, 1), [p1, k3] 2 (2, 4, 4) times, p1, k1 (2, 0, 1), M1R-P; sm, p3, sm; M1L-P, k1 (2, 0, 1), [p1, k3] 6 (6, 8, 8) times, p1, k1 (2, 0, 1), M1R-P; sm, p3, sm; M1L-P, k1 (2, 0, 1), [p1, k3] 2 (2, 4, 4) times, p1, k1 (2, 0, 1), M1R-P; sm, p3, sm; M1L-P, k0 (0, 0, 1), p0 (0, 1, 1), k0 (1, 2, 2), [k1, p1] 3 times, edge st—83 (91, 107, 115) sts.

Beg with Row 3, follow charts for right front, sleeve, back, sleeve and left front for specified sts, beg and ending where indicated for size being worked and working 3 raglan sts in pat established on Rows 1 and 2; continue to inc at raglan edges of fronts, sleeves and back [every WS row] 14 more times, working new sts in Flowery Rib pat as they accumulate, ending with a WS row—195 (203, 219, 227) sts with 22 (23, 25, 26) sts each front, 41 (43, 47, 49) sts each sleeve and 57 (59, 63, 65) back sts.

Join Yoke

Next row (RS): Work in established pat to end of row, then cast on 14 front neck sts; pm for beg of rnd and join—209 (217, 233, 241) sts.

Shape Raglan

Rnd 1 (inc): Continue in established pats, working new front neck sts in established seed st, and working raglan incs as follows: *work to marker, M1L, sm, work 3 raglan sts, sm, M1R; rep from * around, then work to end—217 (225, 241, 249) sts.

Work 5 more rnds in established pat, working raglan incs every other rnd—233 (241, 257, 265) sts.

Next rnd (inc): Discontinue working seed st at front neck; work in established Flowery Rib pat across all front sts, M1L; sm, k3, sm; M1R, continue working across sleeve, back, sleeve and raglan sts, working raglan incs as established, and working established Flowery Rib pat across front neck sts to last 2 sts, p2tog—240 (248, 264, 272) sts.

Continue in established pat and work raglan incs [every other rnd] 7 (9, 13, 15) more times, ending with an inc rnd—296 (320, 368, 392) sts.

Separate Sleeves from Body

Next Rnd: Removing raglan markers as you come to them and maintaining pat, work 35 (38, 42, 44) sts for right front, transfer next 65 (71, 83, 89) sts to waste yarn for right sleeve, cast on 11 (12, 12, 15) underarm sts, pm for "side seam", cast on 11 (12, 12, 15) underarm sts, work next 83 (89, 101, 107) sts for back, transfer next 65 (71, 83, 89) sts to waste yarn for left sleeve, cast on 11 (12, 12, 15) sts, pm for "side seam", cast on 11 (12, 12, 15) sts, work 48 (51, 59, 63) sts for left front—210 (226, 250, 274) sts.

BODY

Rnd 1: *Work in pat to 1 st before side seam marker, k1, sm, k1; rep from * once, then work in pat to end of rnd.

Work even in pat for 1 (2, 1½, 1½) inches, knitting the sts before and after side seam markers as established.

Dec rnd: *Work to 3 sts before side marker, k2tog, k1, sm, k1, ssk; rep from * once, then work in pat to end of rnd—206 (222, 246, 270) sts.

Work even for 6 rnds.

Rep [last 7 rnds] 4 (4, 5, 5) times—190 (206, 226, 250) sts.

Work even for 1½ inches.

Inc rnd: *Work to 1 st before side marker, M1L, k1, sm, k1, M1R; rep from * once, then work in pat to end of rnd—194 (210, 230, 254) sts.

Work even for 6 rnds.

Rep [last 7 rnds] 4 (4, 5, 5) times—210 (226, 250, 274) sts.

Work even for 1 (1½, ½, 1) inches.

Work even in seed st for 1 inch.

Bind off all sts loosely in pat.

SLEEVES

Transfer 65 (71, 83, 89) sleeve sts from waste yarn to 16-inch size 6 needle.

Rnd 1 (RS): Beg at center underarm, pick up and knit 11 (12, 12, 15) sts, work in established pat to end of rnd, pick up and knit 11 (12, 12, 15) sts, pm for beg of rnd—87 (95, 105, 115) sts.

Next 4 rnds: K1, work in established Flowery Rib pat to 1 st before marker, k1.

Dec rnd: K1, ssk, work in pat to last 3 sts, k2tog, k1—85 (93, 103, 113) sts.

Rep Dec rnd [every 4 rnds] 11 (10, 8, 5) times, then [every other rnd] 4 (8, 14, 21) times—55 (57, 60, 62) sts.

Work even for 4 rnds.

Bind off all sts.

FINISHING

Weave in loose ends. Block to finished measurements.

COLLAR

With WS facing, using size 6 needle, and beg at left front, space pick up and knit 67 (75, 91, 99) sts along neck; do not join.

Work 2 rows in seed stitch.

Change to size 4 needle; work 4 rows even.

Change to size 6 needle; work even until collar measures 2 inches.

Change to size 7 needle; work even 4 rows even.

Bind off loosely in pat.

CUFF

Using provisional method and size 6 dpns, cast on 9 sts; do not join.

Row 1: Edge st, *k1, p1; rep from * to last st, edge st.

Rep Row 1 until piece measures 1½ (1¾, 2, 2¼) inches.

Inc row: Edge st, M1R, work to last st, edge st—10 sts.

Working new sts in established seed st, rep Inc row [every 6 rows] 3 times—13 sts. Work 5 rows even.

Dec row: Edge st, dec 1 in pat, work in pat to last st, edge st—12 sts.

Rep Dec row [every 6 rows] 3 times—9 sts.
Work even for 1½ (1¾, 2, 2¼) inches.
Leave sts on dpn.
Unzip provisional cast-on and transfer live sts to 2nd dpn.
Fold cuff so that dpns are parallel with

RS tog, then join top and bottom sts using 3-Needle Bind-Off.

Block cuffs, then turn RS out. Sew to sleeves using backstitch.

Weave in rem ends. Block collar and cuff seam. ●

STRUCTURE RIB PULLOVER **SCHEMATIC & CHARTS**

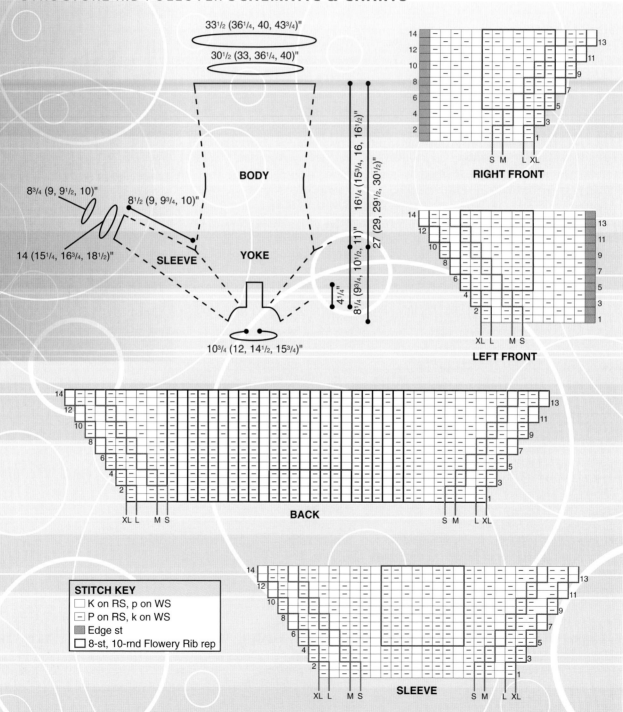

STITCH KEY
☐ K on RS, p on WS
⊟ P on RS, k on WS
▨ Edge st
☐ 8-st, 10-rnd Flowery Rib rep

GONE**downtown**TOP

DESIGN BY SIMONA MERCHANT-DEST

To satisfy your desire for eco-friendly yarns, try this delightful design made with organically-grown cotton.

 INTERMEDIATE

SIZES
Woman's extra-small (small, medium, large, extra-large, 2X-large) Instructions are given for smallest size, with larger sizes in parentheses. When only 1 number is given, it applies to all sizes.

FINISHED MEASUREMENTS
Chest: 33 (35¼, 39¾, 44, 48¼, 52¾) inches
Length: 21 (21, 21½, 21½, 22¼, 22¼) inches

MATERIALS
Blue Sky Alpacas Skinny Dyed (DK weight; 100% organically grown cotton; 150 yds/65g per ball): 6 (6, 7, 7, 8, 9) balls zinc #304
Size 4 (3.50mm) 24-inch (or longer) circular needles or size needed to obtain gauge
Size 5 (3.75mm) 16- and 32-inch (or longer) circular needles or size needed to obtain gauge
Stitch holder (optional)
Removable stitch markers

GAUGE
22 sts and 32 rows = 4 inches/10cm in St st with larger needle.
22 sts and 32 rows = 4 inches/10cm in Lacy Diamonds pat with larger needle.
25 sts and 32 rows = 4 inches/10cm in K3, P2 Rib with smaller needle.
To save time, take time to check gauge.

SPECIAL ABBREVIATIONS
Triple yo: Insert RH needle into next st, wrapping yarn around needle 3 times, complete knit st.

Cluster st: Wyif, slip 5 triple yo sts, dropping extra 2 yo's of triple yo's, [bring yarn to back between needles, sl 5 sts back to LH needle, bring yarn to front between needles, sl 5 sts to RH] twice, bring yarn to back.
Decrease 2 (dec2): Slip next 2 sts 1 at a time pwise, k1, p2sso.

PATTERN STITCHES
Daisy (multiple of 6 sts + 1)
Row 1 (WS): Knit.
Row 2: K1, *[triple yo] 5 times, k1; rep from * to end.
Row 3: K1, *cluster st, k1; rep from * to end.
Row 4: Knit (including each st of cluster).
Row 5: Knit.
Lacy Diamonds (multiple of 6 sts + 1)
Row 1 (RS): *K1, k2tog, yo, k1, yo, ssk; rep from * to last st, k1.
Row 2 and all WS rows: Purl.
Row 3: K2tog, *yo, k3, yo, dec2; rep from * to last 5 sts, yo, k3, yo, ssk.
Row 5: *K1, yo, ssk, k1, k2tog, yo; rep from * to last st, k1.
Row 7: K2, *yo, dec2, yo, k3; rep from * to last 5 sts, yo, dec2, yo, k2.
Row 8: Purl.
Rep Rows 1–8 for pat.

PATTERN NOTES
Top is worked from neck down. Starting with back, stitches are cast on for neck and shoulders/sleeves and worked down toward waist. Front is worked as for back with stitches picked up from back shoulders/sleeves and neck stitches cast on. Waist stitches are picked up from front and back and worked in the round to bottom.

A chart for the Lacy Diamonds pattern is included for those preferring to work from charts.

Schematic waist measurements are for unstretched rib; waist will comfortably stretch to at least 29 (31, 35½, 39½, 43, 47½) inches.

BACK

With larger long circular needle, cast on 139 (145, 157, 169, 181, 193) sts, do not join. Using removable markers, mark 36th (39th, 42nd, 49th, 54th, 59th) st from each end for neck.

***Row 1 (WS):** Knit.
Row 2 (RS): Purl.
Row 3: Knit.
Row 4: Knit.
Row 5: Purl.
Row 6: Knit.

Rep last 2 rows 1 (1, 2, 2, 2, 2) more time(s).
Work 5-row Daisy pat.
Work 6 (6, 6, 6, 8, 8) rows in St st.
Next Row (RS): Purl.
Next Row: Knit.
Next Row: Purl.^^^
Next Row: Purl.

Work 16 rows (2 reps) Lacy Diamonds pat.
Next Row (RS): Knit.****

Work from *** to **** once more and *at the same* time when piece measures approx 8 (8, 8½, 8½, 9, 9) inches from beg, bind off 24 sleeve sts at beg of next 2 rows, then complete the specified rows—91 (97, 109, 121, 133, 145) sts.

Work from *** to ^^^ once more.
Transfer sts to waste yarn or stitch holder.

FRONT

With RS of back facing and using larger needle, beg at top left sleeve, pick up and knit 36 (39, 42, 49, 54, 59) sts along the cast-on edge to marked st; turn work to WS and using knit-on method, cast on 67 (67, 69, 71, 73, 75) front neck sts; turn back to RS and beg at next marked st, pick up and knit 36 (39, 42, 49, 54, 59) sts along the cast-on edge to end—139 (145, 157, 169, 181, 193) sts.

Work as for back, but leave sts on needle—91 (97, 109, 121, 133, 145) sts.

WAIST

With RS facing, transfer back sts to needle.
Joining rnd: *Knit back sts and dec 1 (2, 2, 1, 1, 0) st(s) evenly across; rep from * for front sts—180 (190, 215, 240, 265, 290) sts.

Change to smaller needle and work K3, P2 Rib for 8 inches.
Bind off loosely in rib.

FINISHING

Sew side and underarm sleeve seams.

SLEEVE EDGING

With RS facing and larger needle, beg at sleeve seam, pick up and knit 90 (90, 95, 95, 100, 100) sts along sleeve edge, place marker for beg of rnd.
Purl 3 rnds.
Knit 1 rnd.
Work 5 rnds in K3, P2 Rib.
Bind off loosely in rib.
Weave in all ends. Block to finished measurements. ●

GONE DOWNTOWN TOP SCHEMATIC & CHART

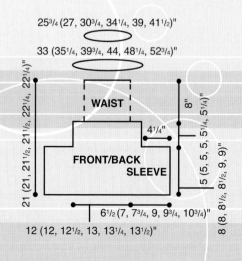

Lacy Diamonds

STITCH KEY
☐ K on RS, p on WS
☑ K2tog
◉ Yo
☒ K2tog-tbl
☒ Dec2

MOCK**mobius**COWL

DESIGN BY ANN SQUIRE

This cozy cowl "with a twist" can be worn in a multitude of ways: untwist and double it around your neck or keep the twist for decorative impact!

 EASY

FINISHED MEASUREMENTS
Circumference: 48 inches
Width: 9 inches

MATERIALS
Misti Alpaca Chunky (bulky
   weight; 100% baby alpaca;
   108 yds/100g per hank): 2 hanks sage
   #VR1380
Size 11 (8mm) 36-inch circular needle or
   size needed to obtain gauge
Stitch marker, 1 in CC for beg of rnd

5 BULKY

GAUGE
10½ sts and 15 rnds = 4 inches/10cm in St st.
16 sts and 16 rnds = 4 inches/10cm in pat st.
To save time, take time to check gauge.

PATTERN STITCHES
Garter stitch (any number of sts)
Rnd 1: Knit.
Rnd 2: Purl.
   Rep Rnds 1 and 2 for pat.

Faggotting (even number of sts)
Rnd 1: *K2tog, yo; rep from * around.
   Rep Rnd 1 for pat.

COWL
Cast on 100 sts.
   Grasp one end of cast-on sts and rotate once around needle to create a full twist in the line of sts; place marker for beg of rnd and join.
   Work 6 rnds garter st.
   Work 20 rnds Faggotting pat.
   Beg with a purl rnd, work 6 rnds garter st.
   Bind off purlwise.

FINISHING
Weave in ends. Block as desired. ●

SHELLtote

DESIGN BY LOIS S. YOUNG

Step out in style with this perfect-size tote for any occasion.

 INTERMEDIATE

FINISHED SIZE
14 inches wide x 12 inches deep

MATERIALS
Blue Sky Alpacas Worsted Hand
  Dyes (worsted weight; 50% royal
  alpaca/50% merino; 100 yds/100g per
  skein): 3 skeins rusty orange #2010
Size 9 (5.5mm) 29-inch circular needle or
  size needed to obtain gauge
Spare needle for 3-Needle Bind-Off
Stitch marker
Stitch holders
½ yard of fabric for lining

GAUGE
16 sts and 24 rows = 4 inches/10cm in Shell pat.
To save time, take time to check gauge.

SPECIAL ABBREVIATIONS
E-Wrap Right (e-R): Inc 1 st by putting twisted
loop on RH needle so that strand crossing on
top leans right.
E-Wrap Left (e-L): Inc 1 st by putting twisted
loop on RH needle so that strand crossing on
top leans left.

PATTERN STITCHES
Shell Pat (worked back and forth) (13 sts)
Rows 1 and 5 (RS): K1, p3, k5, p3, k1.
Row 2 and all WS rows: K4, p5, k4.
Row 3: K1, p3, e-R, k1, p3tog, k1, e-L, p3, k1.
Row 6: Rep Row 2.
Rep Rows 1–6 for pat.

Shell Pat (in the round) (multiple of 8 sts)
Rnds 1, 2, 4, 5: *P2, k5, p1; rep from * around.
Rnd 3: *P2, e-R, k1, p3tog, k1, e-L, p1; rep from
* around.

Rnd 6: Rep Rnd 1.
Rep Rnds 1–6 for pat.

PATTERN NOTE
Handle is worked from the center down, then
stitches are cast on for the sides of the bag; the
rest of the tote is worked in the round. Both
sides are bound off together at the bottom.
The lining is constructed from coordinating
fabric and hand-sewn into the bag.

TOTE
First half of handle
Cast on 13 sts.
  Work 7 reps of 6-row Shell pat, then rep
Rows 1 and 2.
Next row: Work Row 3 and inc 1 st after first st
and before last st—15 sts.
  Work Rows 4 and 5, working 2 new sts in St st.
  Cut yarn leaving a 3-inch tail; transfer sts to
holder.

Second half of handle
With RS facing, pick up and knit 13 sts along
cast-on edge of handle.
  Complete as for first half.

BAG
[Cast on 41 sts, transfer handle sts from holder
to LH needle and work 15 sts in established
pat] twice—112 sts; place marker for beg of rnd
and join.
  Work 11 reps of 6-rnd Shell pat.
  Purl first 21 sts of next rnd to get to side
edge.
  Turn tube inside out; join sides of tube using
3-Needle Bind-Off to close bottom of bag.
  Weave in loose ends; block to finished
measurements.

LINING

Preshrink fabric.

Cut two 17 x 13-inch rectangles. Trace one half of handle on paper, from top to point where it meets bag. Add ½-inch seam allowance to each edge. Cut two pieces using pattern. With RS of fabric tog, seam bottom, sides and handle-top linings.

Sew handle linings to bag lining and press seams open.

Turn under ½-inch on all raw edges.

With RS facing, insert lining into bag and using small running sts, sew edges of lining to bag; tack handle-lining to handle ¼-inch from edge. ●

LISTADO **lace** COWL

DESIGN BY LAURA NELKIN

You'll love this fast and easy-to-make cowl. Wear it as a slouchy neck warmer or as an elegant head covering.

EASY

FINISHED MEASUREMENTS
Circumference: 24 inches
Length: 18 inches

MATERIALS
Schaefer Yarn Heather (fingering weight; 55% merino wool superwash/30% cultivated silk/15% nylon; 400 yds/4 oz per skein): 1 skein Julia Child
Size 7 (4.5mm) 16-inch circular needle or size needed to obtain gauge
Stitch markers, 1 in CC for beg of rnd

1 SUPER FINE

GAUGE
18 sts and 19 rnds = 4 inches/10cm in pat st, blocked.
To save time, take time to check gauge.

PATTERN STITCH
Lacy Rib (multiple of 11 sts)
Rnd 1: *[K2tog, yo] 3 times, k5; rep from * around.
Rnd 2: Knit.

Rnd 3: *K1, [k2tog, yo] twice, k6; rep from * around.
Rnd 4: Knit.
  Rep Rnds 1–4 for pat.

PATTERN NOTES
A chart for the Lacy Rib pattern is included for those preferring to work from charts.
  To make it easier to catch errors you might make working the stitch pattern, place markers every 11 stitches.

COWL
Using knit-on method, cast on 110 sts; place marker for beg of rnd and join, taking care not to twist sts.
  Knit 1 rnd.
Edging rnd: *K2tog, yo; rep from * around.
  Rep Edging rnd once more.
  Rep [Rows 1–4 of Lacy Rib pat] 21 times or to desired length.
  Rep Rnd 1.
Next 2 rnds: Rep Edging rnd.
  Knit 1 rnd.
  Bind off loosely.

FINISHING
Weave in ends. Block lightly. ●

LISTADO LACE COWL **CHART**

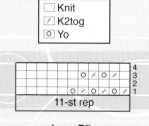

STITCH KEY
☐ Knit
☑ K2tog
☐ Yo

11-st rep

Lacy Rib

SLIP**stitch**SACK

DESIGN BY LISA ELLIS

A classic style with slip stitch construction makes for a dense and sturdy purse.

 INTERMEDIATE

FINISHED SIZE
9 inches wide x 9 ½ inches high (excluding handles)

MATERIALS
Mirasol Sulka (worsted weight; 60% merino wool/20% alpaca/ 20% silk; 55 yds/50g per ball): 2 balls paprika #208 (A), 1 ball each lime #202 (B) and cocoa #204 (C)
2 yds of sport weight wool yarn to match A
Size 10 (6mm) double-point needles (set of 4)
Size 10½ (6.5mm) double-point (set of 5) and 16-inch circular needles or size needed to obtain gauge
Size K/10½ (6.5mm) crochet hook
Open-coil stitch markers
Cardboard (optional)
1 set of closed Shibui Knits square handles (4½ x 5 inches)

GAUGE
21 sts and 36 rnds/rows = 4 inches/10cm in Slip st pat with larger needle.
16 sts and 23 rows = 4 inches/10cm in St st with larger needle.
To save time, take time to check gauge.

SPECIAL TECHNIQUES
3-Needle Bind-Off: With RS tog and needles parallel, using a 3rd needle, knit tog a st from the front needle with 1 from the back. *Knit tog a st from the front and back needles, and slip the first st over the 2nd to bind off. Rep from * around, then fasten off last st.
Provisional Cast-On: With crochet hook and waste yarn, make a chain several sts longer than desired cast on. With knitting needle and project yarn, pick up indicated number of sts in the "bumps" on back of chain. When indicated in pattern, "unzip" the crochet chain to free live sts.

PATTERN STITCHES
Slip Stitch (worked in round on even number of sts)
Rnds 1 and 3: With A, *k1, sl 1; rep from * around.
Rnds 2 and 4: With B, *sl 1, k1; rep from * around.
Rnds 5 and 7: With C, rep Rnd 1.
Rnds 6 and 8: With A, rep Rnd 2.
Rnds 9 and 11: With B, rep Rnd 1.
Rnds 10 and 12: With C, rep Rnd 2.
Rep Rnds 1–12 for pat.

Slip Stitch (worked back and forth on even number of sts)
Row 1 (RS): With A, *k1, sl 1; rep from * to end. Do not turn; slide sts back to other end of needle.
Row 2 (RS): With B, *sl 1, k1; rep from * to end. Turn.
Row 3 (WS): With A, *sl 1, p1; rep from * to end. Do not turn; slide sts back to other end of needle.
Row 4 (WS): With B, *p1, k1; rep from * to end. Turn.
Rows 5 and 7: With C, rep Rows 1 and 3.
Rows 6 and 8: With A, rep Rows 2 and 4.
Rows 9 and 11: With B, rep Rows 1 and 3.
Rows 10 and 12: With C, rep Rows 2 and 4.
Rep Rows 1–12 for pat.

PATTERN NOTES
The bag is worked from the top down; bottom is worked back and forth. Pieces are joined using 3-Needle Bind-Off.

Carry colors not in use up side of work; do not cut.

When working pattern stitch back and forth, right side rows are worked twice, then wrong side rows are worked twice. To do this, after finishing first right side/wrong side row, slide stitches back to the other end of the needle without turning the work.

PURSE

With larger dpns and A, cast on 80 sts; place marker for beg of rnd and join, taking care not to twist sts.

Knit 3 rnds.

Next rnd: Inc 10 sts evenly around—90 sts.

Turning rnd: *P14, mark next st with open-coil st marker, p15, mark next st with open-coil st marker, p14; rep from * around.

Knit 1 rnd.

Work 7 reps of 12-rnd Slip St pat, ending with Rnd 1.

Cut all 3 yarns.

Rearrange sts on smaller dpns to form a rectangle as follows: place last 7 sts (before marker) and first 8 sts (after marker) onto 1 dpn; next 30 sts on 2nd dpn; next 15 sts on 3rd dpn; rem 30 sts on 4th dpn. Set aside.

BOTTOM

With larger dpn and A, using provisional method, cast on 30 sts.

Work 2 reps of 12-row Slip St pat back and forth, then work Rows 1 and 2 once more. Cut colors B and C only. Piece should measure 3 inches. Do not bind off.

Unzip provisional cast-on and place the 30 live sts onto a 2nd dpn. With a 3rd dpn, pick up (do not knit) 15 sts along the edge of the flat bottom and with a 4th dpn, pick up (do not knit) the last 15 sts of the flat bottom edge to form a rectangle.

FINISHING

Join Tube and Bottom

Turn tube inside out.

With larger dpn and A, join Tube and Bottom using 3-Needle Bind-Off.

HEM

Using a tapestry needle and the sport weight wool yarn, sew cast-on edge of purse to the WS, folding at Turning rnd.

Optional: Cut a piece of cardboard to same dimensions as bottom and place inside to keep bottom flat. If desired, line the purse with fabric and sew in place.

HANDLE STRAPS

With smaller dpn and A, removing markers, pick up and knit marked center 17 sts on one side of Turning rnd.

Work 3 inches in St st.

Bind off all sts loosely.

Pull strap through the closed handle to secure handle; with a tapestry needle, sew handle strap to WS of Turning rnd.

Rep on other side. ●

DAISY'S**dress**&**cap**

DESIGNS BY SIMONA MERCHANT-DEST

She'll love this adorable all-seasons ensemble.
Perfect to wear alone or with a long-sleeved top
for fall or winter.

◼◼◼▢ INTERMEDIATE

SIZES
Girl's 2 (4, 6, 8, 10) Instructions are given
for smallest size, with larger sizes in
parentheses. When only 1 number is given,
it applies to all sizes.

FINISHED MEASUREMENTS
Chest: 20¾ (23¾, 25¼, 26¾, 28¼) inches
(unstretched)
Length (without straps): 17¾ (20, 22½,
24¾, 27) inches

MATERIALS
RYC Cashsoft DK (DK weight; 57%
    extrafine merino/33% acrylic
    microfiber/10% cashmere; 142 yds/50g
    per ball): 4 (5, 6, 7, 8) balls sweet #00501
Size 5 (3.75mm) 16-inch (or longer) circular
    needle or size needed to obtain gauge
Size 6 (4mm) 16-inch (or longer) circular
    needle or size needed to obtain gauge
Stitch markers

3 LIGHT

DRESS

GAUGE
22 sts and 30 rnds = 4 inches/10cm in St st
with larger needle.
27 sts and 32 rnds = 4 inches/10cm in K3,
P2 Rib with smaller needle.
25 sts and 32 rnds = 4 inches/10cm in K3,
P1 Rib with smaller needle.
To save time, take time to check gauge.

SPECIAL ABBREVIATIONS
Triple yo: Insert RH needle into next st,
wrapping yarn around needle 3 times,
complete knit st.
Cluster st: Wyib, slip 5 triple yo sts, dropping
extra 2 yo's, [bring yarn to front between
needles, sl 5 sts back to LH needle, bring yarn
to back between needles, sl 5 sts back to RH
needle] twice.
Place marker (pm): Place a marker on needle
to separate sections.
Make 1 purlwise (M1P): Insert LH needle
from front to back under the running thread
between the last st worked and next st on RH
needle; purl into the back of resulting loop.
Make 1 (M1): Insert LH needle from front to
back under the running thread between the
last st worked and next st on RH needle; knit
into the back of resulting loop.

PATTERN STITCHES
Daisy pat (multiple of 6 sts)
Rnd 1: Purl.
Rnd 2: *[Triple yo] 5 times, k1; rep from * to end.
Rnd 3: *Cluster st, p1; rep from * to end.
Rnd 4: Knit (including each st of cluster).
Rnd 5: Purl.

Herringbone pat (any number of sts)
Rnd 1: *K2tog-tbl, dropping only first st of the
k2tog-tbl just made and leave the 2nd st on
the LH needle to be worked again; rep from *
to end, knit the last st.
  Rep Rnd 1 for pat.

PATTERN NOTE
Main part of dress is worked in the round from
top down; straps are knit separately and sewn on.

BODY
With larger needle, cast on 138 (156, 168, 180,
186) sts; pm for beg of rnd and join, taking care
not to twist sts.

Work 1 rep of 5-rnd Daisy pat.
Change to smaller needle and knit 1 rnd.
Inc rnd: Knit and inc 2 (4, 2, 0, 4) sts evenly around—140 (160, 170, 180, 190) sts.
Purl 1 rnd.
Work K3, P2 Rib until piece measures approx 3 (3½, 4, 4½, 5) inches.

WAIST
Dec rnd: *[K3, p2] 9 (6, 7, 8, 9) times, [k3, p2tog] 5 (10, 10, 10, 10) times; rep from * once more—130 (140, 150, 160, 170) sts.
Next rnd: *[K3, p2] 9 (6, 7, 8, 9) times, [k3, p1] 5 (10, 10, 10, 10) times; rep from * once more.
Rep last rnd until piece measures approx 5 (6, 7, 8, 9) inches.

HIP
Inc rnd: *[K3, p2] 9 (6, 7, 8, 9) times, [k3, p1, M1P] 5 (10, 10, 10, 10) times; rep from * once more—140 (160, 170, 180, 190) sts.
Work even in K3, P2 Rib until piece measures 6¾ (8, 9½, 10¾, 12) inches.

SKIRT
Change to larger needle.
Work 2 rnds in Herringbone pat.
Knit 1 rnd.
Inc rnd: *K10, M1; rep from * to end—154 (176, 187, 198, 209) sts.
Work even in St st until skirt measures 9½ (10½, 11½, 12½, 13½) inches.
Dec rnd: Knit and dec 4 (2, 1, 0, 5) sts evenly around—150 (174, 186, 198, 204) sts.
Work 1 rep of 5-rnd Daisy pat.
Change to smaller needle.
Knit 3 rnds.
Purl 2 rnds.
Bind off pwise.

SHOULDER STRAPS
Make 2
With smaller needle, cast on 8 sts; do not join.
Row 1 (WS): K2, p4, k2.
Row 2 (RS): K1, p1, k4, p1, k1.
Rep Rows 1 and 2 until strap measures 6½ (7, 7½, 8, 9) inches or desired length.
Bind off.

FINISHING
Lay dress on a flat surface with K3, P1 Rib centered at both back and front. Measure

1¾ (2, 2¼, 2½, 3) inches from each side and place markers for shoulder strap placement at both front and back.

With WS facing, sew each shoulder strap to dress at marked locations at cast-on edge and Rnd 7 (about ¾ inches below cast-on edge) of body.

Weave in all ends. Block garment to finished measurements.

HAT

 INTERMEDIATE

SIZES
Girl's small (medium, large) Instructions are given for smallest size, with larger sizes in parentheses. When only 1 number is given, it applies to all sizes.

FINISHED MEASUREMENTS
Circumference: 18 (19¾, 20½) inches
Height: 6¾ (7½, 8) inches

MATERIALS
RYC Cashsoft DK (DK weight; 57% extrafine merino/33% acrylic microfiber/10% cashmere; 142 yds/50g per ball): 1 ball sweet #00501
Size 5 (3.75mm) 16-inch circular needle or size needed to obtain gauge
Size 6 (4mm) double-point (set of 5) and 16-inch circular needles or size needed to obtain gauge
Stitch markers, 1 in CC for beg of rnd

GAUGE
20 sts and 32 rnds = 4 inches/10cm in Lacy Diamonds pat with smaller needle.
22 sts and 30 rnds = 4 inches/10cm in Daisy pat with larger needle.
22 sts and 30 rnds = 4 inches/10cm in St st with larger needle.
To save time, take time to check gauge.

SPECIAL ABBREVIATIONS
Pass stitch over (pso): Pass last st over first st of rnd; leave first st of rnd on LH needle to be worked in next rnd.
Decrease 2 (dec2): Slip next 2 sts 1 at a time pwise, k1, p2sso.

PATTERN STITCHES

Daisy pat (multiple of 6 sts)
See Dress pat.

Lacy Diamonds (multiple of 6 sts)
Rnd 1: *K1, k2tog, yo, k1, yo, k2tog-tbl; rep from * around.
Rnds 2, 4, 6: Knit.
Rnd 3: K2tog, *yo, k3, yo, dec2; rep from * to last 4 sts, yo, k3, yo, pso.
Rnd 5: *K1, yo, k2tog-tbl, k1, k2tog, yo; rep from * around.
Rnd 7: K2, *yo, dec2, yo, k3; rep from * to last 4 sts, yo, dec2, yo, k1.
Rnd 8: Knit.
Rep Rnds 1–8 for pat.

PATTERN NOTE

Switch to double-point needles when stitches no longer fit comfortably on circular needle.

HEM

With smaller needle, cast on 90 (96,102) sts; pm for beg of rnd and join, taking care not to twist sts.
Purl 3 rnds.

Knit 3 rnds.
Change to larger needle and work 1 rep of 5-rnd Daisy pat.
Change to smaller needle and knit 3 rnds.
Purl 3 rnds.

BODY

Knit 1 rnd.
Work 2 [8-rnd] reps of Lacy Diamonds pat, then work [Rnds 1–4] 0 (1, 1) more time(s).
Purl 3 rnds.

CROWN

Next rnd: *K15 (16, 17), pm; rep from * around.
Change to larger needle.
Dec rnd: *Knit to 2 sts before marker, k2tog; rep from * around—84 (90, 96) sts.
Rep Dec rnd [every other rnd] 3 (3, 5) times, then [every rnd] 9 (10, 9) times—12 sts.
Next rnd: [K2tog] around—6 sts.

FINISH

Cut yarn leaving 10-inch tail. Using tapestry needle, thread tail through rem sts and pull tight to secure.
Weave in all ends. Block. ●

DAISY'S DRESS & CAP SCHEMATIC & CHART

LACY DIAMONDS

6-st rep

STITCH KEY
☐ Knit
☑ K2tog
☐ Yo
☑ K2tog-tbl
☑ Dec2
P pso

DRESS

28 (32, 34, 36, 38)"

17³/₄ (20, 22¹/₂, 24³/₄, 27)"

11 (12, 13, 14, 15)"

6³/₄ (8, 9¹/₂, 10³/₄, 12)"

2³/₄ (3, 3¹/₄, 3¹/₂, 4)"

19 (20¹/₂, 21¹/₂, 23³/₄, 24¹/₄)"

20³/₄ (23³/₄, 25¹/₄, 26³/₄, 28¹/₄)"

BELL-bottomBAMBINI

DESIGN BY LAURA NELKIN

These stylish baby pants are designed with room for a diaper. The wide legs cuff to give added length when your baby grows!

 INTERMEDIATE

SIZES
Infant's newborn (3–9, 9–18, 18–24, 24, 36) months Instructions are given for smallest size, with larger sizes in parentheses. When only 1 number is given, it applies to all sizes.

FINISHED MEASUREMENTS
Waist: approx 13 (15¼, 17, 19, 20¾, 22½) inches
Length: 12½ (14½ 17¾, 20, 22¼, 24½) inches

MATERIALS
Schaefer Yarn Nichole (sock weight; 80% extrafine superwash merino wool/20% nylon; 405 yds/5 oz per skein): 1 (1, 1, 2, 2, 2) skein(s) Greenjeans

Size 3 (3.25mm) 16-inch circular needle or one size smaller than needed to obtain gauge

Size 4 (3.5mm) double-point (set of 5) and 16-inch (for 3 smaller sizes) or 24-inch (for 3 larger sizes) circular needle or size needed to obtain gauge

Stitch markers, 1 in CC for beg of rnd

1-inch-wide elastic, 13½ (15¾, 17½, 19½, 21¼, 23) inches long

GAUGE
22 sts and 32 rnds = 4 inches/10cm in St st with larger needle.
To save time, take time to check gauge.

SPECIAL ABBREVIATIONS
Place marker (pm): Place a marker on needle to separate sections.

Make 1 Left (M1L): Insert LH needle from front to back under the running thread between the last st worked and next st on LH needle; knit into the back of resulting loop.

Make 1 Right (M1R): Insert LH needle from back to front under the running thread between the last st worked and next st on LH needle. With RH needle, knit into the front of resulting loop.

Knit in front and back of stitch (kfb): Inc by knitting in front loop, then in back loop of st.

Wrap and Turn (W&T): Bring yarn to RS of work between needles, slip next st pwise to RH needle, bring yarn around this st to WS, slip st back to LH needle, turn work to begin working back in the other direction.

SPECIAL TECHNIQUES
Hiding wraps: Pick up wrap from front to back and knit tog with wrapped st.

PATTERN NOTES
Pants are worked in one piece from the top down; the seat is shaped using short rows and there is a crotch gusset.

Beginning of round marker is at left side seam.

Change to double-point needles as necessary for legs.

PANTS
WAISTBAND
With smaller needle, cast on 80 (90, 100, 110, 120, 130) sts; pm for beg of rnd and join, taking care not to twist sts.

Knit 9 rnds.
Turning rnd: Purl.
Change to larger needle.
Next 10 rnds: K2, *p2, k3; rep from * to last 3 sts, p2, k1.

Next rnd: K2, p2, k33 (38, 43, 48, 53, 58), p2, k3, p2, knit to last 3 sts, p2, k1.

Next rnd (inc): K2, p2, *k7 (6, 6, 7, 7, 8), kfb; rep from * 3 (4, 5, 5, 5, 5) more times, k1 (3, 1, 0, 5, 4), p2, k1; rep from * once more—88 (100, 112, 122, 132, 142) sts.

Work even until piece measures 2¼ (2¼, 3, 3, 3, 3) inches from Turning rnd.

Shaping the seat

Note: Maintain the rib as established at side seams throughout, with rem sts worked in St st.

Short Row 1 (RS): Work 4 sts, k36 (42, 48, 53, 58, 63); W&T.

Short Row 2: P35 (41, 47, 52, 57, 62); W&T.

Work 4 (6, 6, 8, 10, 12) rnds even, hiding wrapped sts as you come to them on the first rnd.

Short Row 3: Work 4 sts, k34 (40, 46, 51, 56, 61); W&T.

Short Row 4: P31 (37, 43, 48, 53, 58); W&T.

Work 4 (6, 6, 8, 10, 12) rnds even, hiding wrapped sts as you come to them on the first rnd.

Short Row 5: Work 4 sts, k32 (38, 44, 49, 54, 59); W&T.

Short Row 6: P27 (33, 39, 44, 49, 54); W&T.

Work 4 (6, 6, 8, 10, 12) rnds even, hiding wrapped sts as you come to them on the first rnd.

Short Row 7: Work 4 sts, k30 (36, 42, 47, 52, 57); W&T.

Short Row 8: P23 (29, 35, 40, 45, 50); W&T.

Work 4 (6, 6, 8, 10, 12) rnds even, hiding wrapped sts as you come to them on the first rnd.

Short Row 9: Work 4 sts, k28 (34, 40, 45, 50, 55); W&T.

Short Row 10: P19 (25, 31, 36, 41, 46); W&T.

Work even until front measures 4½ (5½, 6½, 7½, 8½, 9½) inches from waist ribbing; the back should measure approx 6 (7, 8, 9, 10, 11) inches.

GUSSET

Set-up rnd: *Work 4, k18 (21, 24, 26, 29, 31) pm, k1 (1, 1, 2, 1, 2), pm, k18 (21, 24, 26, 29, 31), work 3; rep from * once more.

Rnd 1: *Work 4, k18 (21, 24, 26, 29, 31), slip marker, M1R, k1 (1, 1, 2, 1, 2), M1L, slip marker, k18 (21, 24, 26, 29, 31), work 3; rep from * once more.

Rnd 2: Knit around.

Rep last 2 rnds 4 (4, 5, 5, 6, 6) times more—11 (11, 13, 14, 15, 16) sts for each gusset section and 43 (49, 55, 59, 65, 69) sts for each leg.

Work to first gusset marker, slip marker, knit across first set of gusset sts, cut yarn leaving a 24-inch tail. Remove next marker and transfer first set of leg sts onto 3 dpns. Remove next marker. Fold circular needle in half so that the WS of the gussets are tog, then graft gusset sts tog using Kitchener st.

Leave 2nd set of leg sts on circular needle.

LEGS

Join yarn for first leg and work around and then pick up 2 (2, 2, 3, 3, 3) sts tbl from the sides of the gusset area, pm, and join into rnd—45 (51, 57, 62, 68, 72) sts.

Work around for 1 (1½, 1½, 2, 2, 2½) inch(es).

Bell Bottom Shaping

Inc rnd: Knit to purl sts, M1R, p2, k3, p2, M1L, knit to end of rnd.

Work 5 (5, 7, 9, 10, 11) rnds.

Work last 6 (6, 8, 10, 11, 12) rnds 4 times more—55 (61, 67, 72, 78, 82) sts

Set-up rnd (inc): Knit to side seam sts and inc 0 (2, 1, 1, 1, 1) st(s) evenly across, work side seam sts, knit to end and inc 0 (2, 2, 2, 1, 2) st(s) evenly across—55 (65, 70, 75, 80, 85) sts

Next rnd: *P2, k3; rep from * around.

Work even in established rib for 1 (1½, 1½, 1½, 2, 2) inch(es).

Bind off loosely in rib.

FINISHING

Weave in ends. Block to finished measurements.

WAISTBAND

Fold waistband to inside at turning row and whipstitch down, leaving a hole for the elastic. Take a piece of elastic the correct length for the size you are making and thread through the casing, making sure not to twist it. Overlap ends by ½ inch and sew to secure. Finish whipstitching casing. ●

BELL-BOTTOM BAMBINI SCHEMATIC

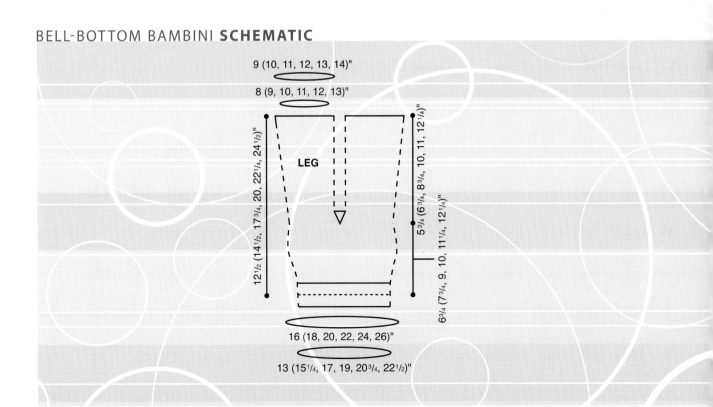

TULIP**lace**TUNIC**and**HAT

DESIGNS BY SIMONA MERCHANT-DEST

This sweet lacy tunic can be worn by itself, or paired with a vest over a long-sleeve tee.

 **INTERMEDIATE**

SIZES

Girl's 2 (4, 6, 8, 10) Instructions are given for smallest size, with larger sizes in parentheses. When only 1 number is given, it applies to all sizes.

FINISHED MEASUREMENTS

Chest: 21 (23, 25, 27, 29) inches (buttoned)
Length: 15¾ (17¼, 19¼, 21¼, 22) inches

MATERIALS

Nashua Handknits Creative Focus
   Cotton DK (DK weight; 100%
   Egyptian mercerized cotton; 118 yds/50g
   per ball): 3 (4, 5, 6, 6) balls lavender #0182
   for top; 1 (2) balls lavender #0182 for hat
Size 5 (3.75mm) double-point (set of 5) and
   24-inch (or longer) circular needles or
   size needed to obtain gauge
Stitch holders
Stitch markers
3 (3, 3, 4, 4) ½-inch buttons

3 LIGHT

GAUGE

22 sts and 28 rows/rnds = 4 inches/10cm in St st.
21 sts and 30 rows/rnds = 4 inches/10cm in
Tulip Lace pat.
To save time, take time to check gauge.

SPECIAL ABBREVIATIONS

Place marker (pm): Place a marker on needle to separate sections.
Make 1 Purlwise (M1P): Insert LH needle from front to back under the running thread between the last st worked and next st on LH needle; purl into the back of resulting loop.
Make 1 Left (M1L): Insert LH needle from front to back under the running thread between the last st worked and next st on LH needle; knit into the back of resulting loop.
Make 1 Right (M1R): Insert LH needle from back to front under the running thread between the last st worked and next st on LH needle. With RH needle, knit into the front of resulting loop.

PATTERN STITCHES

Tulip Lace (multiple of 8 sts + 7)
Row 1 (RS): Knit.
Row 2 and all WS row: Purl.
Row 3: K3, *yo, ssk, k6; rep from * to last 4 sts, yo, ssk, k2.
Row 5: K1, *k2tog, yo, k1, yo, ssk, k3; rep from * to last 6 sts, k2tog, yo, k1, yo, ssk, k1.
Row 7: Rep Row 3.
Row 9: Knit.
Row 11: K7, *yo, ssk, k6; rep from * to end.
Row 13: K5, *k2tog, yo, k1, yo, ssk, k3; rep from * to last 2 sts, k2.
Row 15: Rep Row 11.
Row 16: Rep Row 2.
Rep Rows 1–16 for pat.

K2, P2 Rib (multiple of 4 sts + 2)
Row 1 (WS): P2, *k2, p2; rep from * to end.
Row 2: K2, *p2, k2; rep from * to end.
Rep Rows 1 and 2 for pat.

PATTERN NOTES

Top is worked from neck down in one piece to underarms, at which point it is divided for sleeves and lower body. The body is worked in one piece downward. Each sleeve is finished in the round.

Use knit-on or cable method to cast on new stitches within pattern.

A chart for the Tulip Lace pattern is included for those preferring to work from charts.

SWEATER

YOKE

With circular needle, cast on 77 (81, 81, 85, 85) sts; do not join in round.

Row 1 (RS): Purl.

Row 2: K10 (11, 11, 12, 12) front sts, pm, k16 sleeve sts, pm, 25 (27, 27, 29, 29) back sts, pm, k16 sleeve sts, pm, k10 (11, 11, 12, 12) front sts.

Row 3 (inc): *Purl to 1 st before marker, M1P, p1, slip marker, p1, M1P; rep from * 3 times, purl to end—85 (89, 89, 93, 93) sts.

Row 4: Knit.

Row 5 (inc): *Knit to 1 st before marker, M1R, k1, slip marker, k1, M1L; rep from * 3 times, knit to end—93 (97, 97, 101, 101) sts.

Row 6: Purl.

Rep [last 2 rows] 14 (16, 17, 18, 19) times—205 (225, 233, 245, 253) sts with 26 (29, 30, 32, 33) front sts, 48 (52, 54, 56, 58) sleeve sts and 57 (63, 65, 69, 71) back sts.

Divide for sleeves and body

Next row (RS): Removing markers as you come to them, *knit to marker, place 48 (52, 54, 56, 58) sleeve sts onto a holder, cast on 0 (0, 4, 6, 8) sts for underarm; rep from * once more, knit to end—109 (121, 133, 145, 153) sts on working needle (both fronts and back) and 48 (52, 54, 56, 58) sts on hold for each sleeve.

BODY

Next row (WS): Purl.

Work 6 (8, 10, 12, 16) rows in St st.

Work 3 rows in Rev St st.

Next row (inc): Purl inc 6 (11, 6, 10, 10) sts evenly spaced across—115 (131, 139, 155, 163) sts.

SKIRT

Row 1 (RS): K1, p1, pm, work Row 1 of Tulip Lace to last 2 sts, pm, p1, k1.

Row 2: P2, work Row 2 of Tulip Lace to last 2 sts, p2.

Maintaining first and last 2 sts in established pat, work even in Tulip Lace until skirt measures approx 9¼ (10¼, 11½, 12½, 12½) inches, ending with Row 8 or 16 of pat.

Edging

Work 2 rows in St st.

Work 3 rows in Rev St st.

Next row (WS): Knit and bind off all sts.

SLEEVES

Transfer sleeve sts from holder to 4 dpns.

Set-up rnd (RS): With new dpn, beg in center underarm, pick up and knit 0 (0, 2, 3, 4) sts, knit across sleeves sts, pick up and knit 0 (0, 2, 3, 4) sts, pm for beg of rnd and join—48 (52, 58, 62, 66) sts.

Purl 3 rnds.

Bind off all sts pwise.

Button Band

With RS facing and using circular needle, pick up and knit 34 (42, 42, 46, 50) sts along left front edge, beg at neck and ending at last Rev St st row of yoke.

Work 5 rows in K2, P2 Rib.
Bind off all sts in pat.

Buttonhole Band

Place 3 (3, 3, 4, 4) markers along right front
edge between neck and last Rev St st row of
yoke to indicate button placement.

With RS facing and using circular needle,
pick up and knit 34 (42, 42, 46, 50) sts along
right front edge, beg at last Rev St st of yoke
and ending at neck.

Row 1 (WS): Work in K2, P2 Rib.

Row 2 (buttonhole): Work in established rib
and bind off 2 sts at each buttonhole marker.

Row 3: Work in established rib and work
double-yo over each set of bound-off sts.

Row 4: Work in established rib and work 2 sts
tbl in established rib each double-yo.

Rows 5 and 6: Work rib.
Bind off all sts in pat.

FINISHING

Sew buttons onto left front edge opposite
buttonholes. Weave in all ends. Block to
finished measurements.

HAT

SIZES

Girls' small (medium) Instructions are given for
smaller size, with larger size in parentheses.
When only 1 number is given, it applies to both
sizes.

FINISHED MEASUREMENTS

Circumference: 18¼ (19¾) inches
Length: 7 (8) inches

PATTERN STITCH

Tulip Lace (multiple of 8 sts)

Rnd 1 (RS): Knit.

Rnd 2 and all even-number rnds: Knit.

Rnd 3: *K3, yo, ssk, k3; rep from * around.

Rnd 5: *K1, k2tog, yo, k1, yo, ssk, k2; rep from *
around.

Rnd 7: Rep Rnd 3.

Rnd 9: Knit to 1 st before beg of rnd marker,
pm (new beg of rnd for next 8 rnds), remove
previous marker on next rnd.

Rnd 11: Yo, ssk, k3, *k3, yo, ssk, k3; rep from *
to last 3 sts, k3.

Rnd 13: K1, yo, ssk, k2, *k1, k2tog, yo, k1, yo, ssk,
k2; rep from * to last 3 sts, k1, k2tog, yo.

Rnd 15: Rep Rnd 11.

Rnd 16: Rep Rnd 2 to beg of rnd marker,
remove marker, k1, pm for new beg for next
8 rnds.
Rep Rnds 1–16 for pat.

PATTERN NOTES

Hat is worked from bottom edge to crown.

For Tulip Lace, the marker indicating the
beginning of the round is shifted over 1 stitch
every 8 rounds because the pattern shifts
position (see Tulip Lace pattern).

Change to double-point needles when
stitches no longer fit comfortably on circular
needle.

A chart for the Tulip Lace pattern is included
for those preferring to work from charts.

BOTTOM

With circular needle, cast on 96 (104) sts;
pm for beg of rnd and join, taking care not to
twist sts.
Purl 4 rnds.

Work 32 (40) rnds in Tulip Lace pat.
Knit 1 rnd.

CROWN
Next rnd: *K12 (13), pm; rep from * around.
Dec rnd: *Knit to 2 sts before marker, k2tog;
rep from * around—88 (94) sts.
Next rnd: Knit 1 rnd.
   Rep [last 2 rnds] 3 times—64 (72) sts.
   Rep Dec rnd only 6 (7) times—16 sts.
Next rnd: K2tog around—8 sts.

FINISHING
Cut yarn, leaving a 5-inch tail. Using tapestry
needle, thread tail through rem sts, and
pull tight.
   Weave in all ends. Block as necessary. ●

EASY ONE-PIECE CARDIGAN **SCHEMATIC & CHARTS**

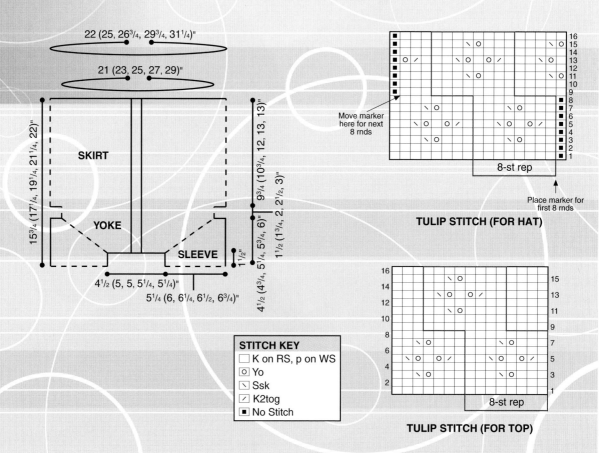

22 (25, 26³/₄, 29³/₄, 31¹/₄)"

21 (23, 25, 27, 29)"

SKIRT

15³/₄ (17¹/₄, 19¹/₄, 21¹/₄, 22)"

YOKE

SLEEVE

1¹/₂"

4¹/₂ (5, 5, 5¹/₄, 5¹/₄)"

5¹/₄ (6, 6¹/₄, 6¹/₂, 6³/₄)"

9³/₄ (10³/₄, 12, 13, 13)"

4¹/₂ (4³/₄, 5¹/₄, 5³/₄, 6)"

1¹/₂ (1³/₄, 2, 2¹/₂, 3)"

Move marker
here for next
8 rnds

8-st rep

Place marker for
first 8 rnds

TULIP STITCH (FOR HAT)

STITCH KEY
☐ K on RS, p on WS
⊡ Yo
◹ Ssk
◿ K2tog
▪ No Stitch

8-st rep

TULIP STITCH (FOR TOP)

TOTALLY**seamless**JUMPER

DESIGN BY PAULINE SCHULTZ

What a sweetie pie she'll be in this cute-as-a-button jumper!

 EASY

SIZES
Child's 12 months (18 months, 2 years, 3 years, 4 years) Instructions are given for smallest size, with larger sizes in parentheses. When only one number is given, it applies to all sizes.

FINISHED MEASUREMENTS
Chest: 20 (21, 22, 23, 24) inches
Length: 20 (21½, 23, 24½, 26) inches

MATERIALS
Schaefer Yarn Miss Priss (worsted weight; 100% merino wool; 280 yds/4 oz per skein): 3 (3, 4, 4, 4) skeins Peter
Size 7 (4.5mm) 24-inch circular needle or size needed to obtain gauge.
Size 8 (5mm) 24-inch circular needle or size needed to obtain gauge
Stitch markers, 1 in CC for beg of rnd
Long stitch holders (optional)
2 novelty buttons

GAUGE
20 sts and 32 rnds = 4 inches/10cm in Mock Cable Garter Rib with larger needle.
18 sts and 38 rows = 4 inches/10cm in garter st with smaller needle.
To save time, take time to check gauge.

SPECIAL ABBREVIATIONS
Left Slip Twist (LST): Drop the first st to front of work, slip 2nd st to RH needle. Pick up the dropped st pwise with the LH needle, slip the 2nd st back to the LH needle and knit it, slip the dropped st to the RH needle.
Left Slip Twist Decrease (LST dec): Insert RH needle into back of next and 3rd st on LH needle. Slip these sts off the needle leaving the 2nd st at front. Pick up this st with the LH needle. Slip the 2 sts on the RH needle to the LH needle and knit them tog, slip next st to RH needle.
Right Slip Twist (RST): Insert the RH needle pwise into the front of the 2nd st on the LH needle, slip it off the needle tog with the first st. With the LH needle, pick up the dropped st and knit it.
Right Slip Twist Decrease (RST dec): Insert RH needle into front of 2nd st and slip to RH needle, dropping the first st off the LH needle to the back. Pick up the dropped st with the LH needle and work k2tog with the next st.

PATTERN STITCH
Mock Cable Garter Rib (multiple of 8 sts)
Rnd 1: Knit.
Rnd 2: *P4, k4; rep from * around.
Rnd 3: Knit.
Rnd 4: *P4, LST, RST; rep from * around.
Rep Rnds 1–4 for pat.

PATTERN NOTES
This jumper is worked from the bottom up, with the skirt knit in the round. After the waist is complete, the piece is divided into front and back, which are worked back and forth. The back straps are longer than the front straps and are brought forward; the straps are joined with a button sewn between both layers.

To maximize the subtle color changes of hand-painted yarn and avoid slight differences between skeins, work with two skeins at once, alternating strands every 2 rows. When knitting back and forth, change strands 1 stitch in from the edge.

JUMPER
SKIRT
With smaller needle, cast on 200 (208, 216, 224, 232) sts; place marker for beg of rnd and join, taking care not to twist sts.

Purl 4 rnds.

Knit 4 rnds.

Purl 4 rnds.

Change to larger needle and work in Mock Cable Garter Rib pat until piece measures 12½ (13½, 14½, 15½, 16½) inches, ending with Rnd 3.

Next rnd (dec): Sl 1, *p2, LST dec, RST dec; rep from * around, working last dec by removing the marker, working the RST dec, then replacing the marker—150 (156, 162, 168, 174) sts.

Knit 1 rnd.

Next rnd (dec): *P2, [k2tog] twice; rep from * around—100 (104, 108, 112, 116) sts.

WAIST

Change to smaller needle and rev St st.

Next rnd (dec): Purl and dec 10 (10, 8, 8, 8) sts evenly around—90 (94, 100, 104, 108) sts.

Purl 3 rnds.

Work in garter st (knit 1 rnd, purl 1 rnd) until waist measures 3¾ (4, 4¼, 4½, 4¾) inches, ending with a purl rnd.

Divide for front & back

*Bind off 9 (10, 12, 12, 12) sts pwise, k36 (37, 38, 40, 42); rep from * once more.

Transfer front sts to holder or waste yarn.

BACK

Change to larger needle and beg working back and forth.

Work in garter st until armhole measures 2¾ (3, 3¼, 3, 3½, 3¾) inches, ending with a WS row.

Back neck and straps

Discontinue alternating yarns.

Next row (RS): K9 (9, 9, 10, 10), join 2nd ball of yarn and bind off 18 (19, 20, 20, 22) sts pwise, k9 (9, 9, 10, 10).

Working both sides at once with separate balls of yarn, work even in garter st until armholes measure 6 (6¼, 6½, 7, 7¼) inches, ending with a WS row.

Bind off pwise.

FRONT

Transfer front sts back to larger needle with WS facing.

Continue in garter st until armholes measure 1¼ (1½, 1½, 1½, 1¾) inches, ending with a WS row.

Front neck and straps

Discontinue alternating yarns.

Next row (RS): K9 (9, 9, 10, 10), join 2nd ball of yarn and bind off 18 (19, 20, 20, 22) sts pwise, k9 (9, 9, 10, 10).

Working both sides at once with separate balls of yarn, work even in garter st until armholes measure 3¾ (4, 4¼, 4½, 4¾) inches. Bind off pwise.

FINISHING

Weave in all ends. Block to finished measurements.

Fold back straps forward over front straps; sew buttons through both layers to join. ●

TOTALLY SEAMLESS JUMPER **SCHEMATIC**

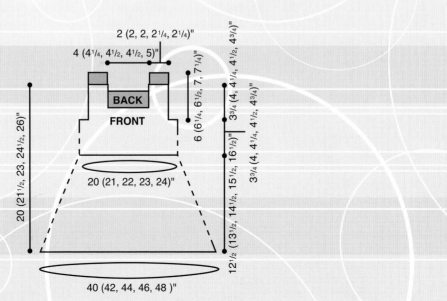

STEPPINGitUPaNOTCH: KNITTINGinNEWdirections

Now we're going to take everything you've learned, and mix it up! This chapter will open a world of knitting that includes side-to-side knitting (also known as working cuff-to-cuff), which is another inventive way to work on circular needles. This construction method allows you to work some portions of your project back and forth and other sections in the round, all in one garment. The possibilities are unlimited!

SPECIAL ways OF working

We've addressed many of the fundamentals of knitting on circular needles in the previous chapters; you can now stretch your imagination and view your projects from a new perspective. In many cases the cast-on edge of a side-to-side garment usually begins at the cuff, which is why this way of working is also known as cuff-to-cuff.

In the example below, we begin our cast-on edge at the left cuff and work back and forth. When the sleeve is complete, stitches are cast on for the front and back, which are worked simultaneously to the back neck, after which they are worked separately to create the front opening. After the neck is complete, right front stitches are cast on, and the back and front are worked simultaneously again. Finally, the right sleeve is worked down to the cuff. In many respects we can compare the benefits of this method of knitting to working in the round because the entire garment is worked in one piece, making the process fluid and less static than other forms of back and forth knitting. Additionally, a back and forth cuff-to-cuff garment is more dynamic than its traditional

"in pieces" counterpart, because you can "try on as you go," instead of making 4 separate body units and hoping for the best. Another benefit to working cuff-to-cuff is that the stitch and color patterns are vertical on the body instead of horizontal, creating a nice slimming effect.

In the next example, both in the round and flat knitting methods are utilized. In the diagram below, the directional arrows indicate that each sleeve and half-yoke is worked separately from the cuff to the center back. After the two pieces are joined at the center, the body is worked in the round from the yoke downward.

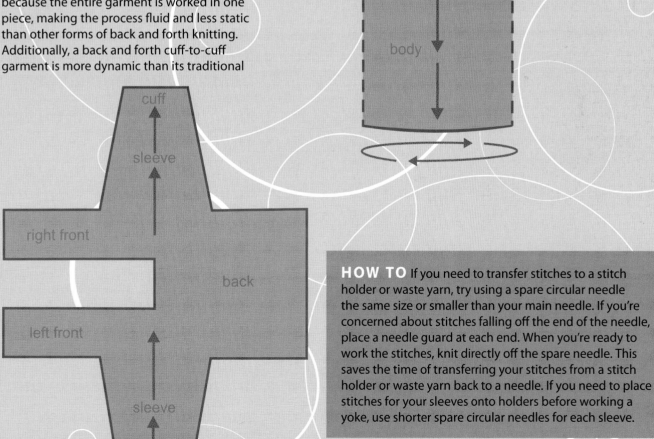

HOW TO If you need to transfer stitches to a stitch holder or waste yarn, try using a spare circular needle the same size or smaller than your main needle. If you're concerned about stitches falling off the end of the needle, place a needle guard at each end. When you're ready to work the stitches, knit directly off the spare needle. This saves the time of transferring your stitches from a stitch holder or waste yarn back to a needle. If you need to place stitches for your sleeves onto holders before working a yoke, use shorter spare circular needles for each sleeve.

SOPHIE'S**shrug**

DESIGN BY LAURA NELKIN

If you're looking to dress up those jeans, this charming shrug will add just the right touch of elegance.

◀▬▬▬▷ INTERMEDIATE

SIZES
Woman's small (medium, large) Instructions are given for smallest size, with larger sizes in parentheses. When only 1 number is given, it applies to all sizes.

FINISHED MEASUREMENTS
Sleeve length to split for back: 9½ (10½, 11½) inches
Body (across back): 18½ (20, 21) inches
Sleeve circumference: 10 (10, 12) inches

MATERIALS
Schaefer Yarn Heather (fingering weight; 55% merino wool superwash/30% silk/15% nylon; 400 yds/4 oz per skein): 1 (2, 2) skeins indigo

1 SUPER FINE

Size 6 (4mm) double-point needles
Size 7 (4.5mm) double-point and 24-inch circular needles or size needed to obtain gauge
Stitch markers, 1 in CC for beg of rnd
966 (1078, 1454) size 6 glass seed beads (optional)
Dental floss threader (optional)

GAUGE
24 sts and 26 rnds = 4 inches/10cm in beaded pat, blocked.
To save time, take time to check gauge.

SPECIAL ABBREVIATIONS
Knit in front and back of stitch (kfb): Inc by knitting in front loop, then in back loop of st.
Purl in front and back of stitch (pfb): Inc by purling in front loop, then in back loop of st.

Place marker (pm): Place a marker on needle to separate sections.

PATTERN STITCHES
Feather and Fan (multiple of 12 sts)
Rnd 1 (RS): *K2tog twice, [yo, k1] 4 times, k2tog twice; rep from * around.
Rnd 2: Purl.
Rnd 3: Knit.
Rep Rnds 1-3 for pat.
Beaded Eyelet Pat (in the round) (multiple of 6 sts)
   Note: The stitch count on the Eyelet pat decreases on Rnds 1 and 3 and is restored to original count on Rnds 2 and 4.
Rnd 1: *Yo with bead, k2tog-tbl, k2, k2tog; rep from * around.
Rnd 2: *Kfb, k4; rep from * around.
Rnd 3: *K1, k2tog, yo with bead, k2tog-tbl, k1; rep from * around.
Rnd 4: *K2, kfb, k2; rep from * around.
   Rep Rnds 1–4 for pat.

Beaded Eyelet Pat (worked back and forth) (multiple of 6 sts + 1)
Row 1 (RS): K1, *yo with bead, k2tog-tbl, k2, k2tog; rep from * across.
Row 2: *Pfb, p4; rep from * to last st, p1.
Row 3: K1, *k1, k2tog, yo with bead, k2tog-tbl, k1; rep from * across.
Row 4: *P2, pfb, p2; rep from * to last st, p1.
   Rep Rows 1–4 for pat.

SPECIAL TECHNIQUES
Yo with bead: As you work yo, slide a bead up the yarn until it touches the RH needle. When you work the next st, the bead will be locked in place.
Getting bead to float at the center top of the yo: This is done on Rnds/Rows 2 and 4

when you are working into the front and back of the yo from the previous row. Hold the bead to the back of the LH needle when working into the front of the st, then slip the bead all the way forward before you work into the back of the st. This "traps" the bead in between the 2 sts perfectly.

3-st Attached I-Cord: *K2, ssk, pick up next st from edge (but do not knit); do not turn. Slip 4 sts back to RH needle; rep from * as instructed.

PATTERN NOTES

This shrug is worked as 2 separate sleeves. Each sleeve is worked in the round, and then split and worked back and forth to center back. The bottom border is applied after the sleeves are grafted together.

After the split for the back, you may need to continue working on double-point needles for a few rows so that there isn't too much stress on the stitches at the edge of the split. You can either continue to keep working on the double-point needles or switch to circular needle, whichever is more comfortable.

The beads are optional.

RIGHT SLEEVE

Thread 483 (539, 727) beads onto yarn.

Using knit-on method and larger dpns, cast on 60 (60, 72) sts; pm for beg of rnd and join, taking care not to twist sts.

Knit 1 rnd.

Work 4 [3-rnd] reps of Feather and Fan.

Work 12 (14, 16) [4-rnd] reps of Beaded Eyelet pat, then work Rnds 1–3 once more.

Note: *Do not place bead on last yo of final rnd.*

Split for armhole and back

Work first 4 sts of pat Rnd 4 (5 sts on RH needle); turn.

Next row (WS): Bind off 10 sts, then beg with p1 (first p1 is already on RH needle from bind-off), work Row 4 of pat across rem sts—49 (49, 61) sts.

Work 14 (15, 16) reps in established Beaded Eyelet pat, ending with p2tog on last row—48 (48, 60) sts.

Cut yarn leaving a 10-inch tail; place sts on waste yarn.

LEFT SLEEVE
Work as for right sleeve; do not cut yarn.

CENTER BACK
Row 1 (RS): *K2tog twice, [yo, k1] 4 times, k2tog twice; rep from * across.
Rows 2 and 3: Knit.
Row 4: *P2tog twice, [yo, p1] 4 times, p2tog twice; rep from * across.
Rows 5 and 6: Purl.
Row 7: *K2tog twice, [yo, k1] 4 times, k2tog twice; rep from * across.
Row 8: Knit.

FINISHING
Transfer right sleeve sts onto a needle.
With RS facing, join pieces using Kitchener st.

BOTTOM EDGING
Beg at bottom edge of right sleeve split (where bound-off sts end), pick up and knit 108 (120, 132) sts evenly across the back, ending at bind-off for left sleeve.
Row 1 (RS): K1, ssk, k9, *k2tog twice, [yo, k1] 4 times, k2tog twice; rep from * to last 12 sts,

k9, k2tog, k1—106 (118, 130) sts.
Rows 2 and 3: K1, ssk, knit to last 3 sts, k2tog, k1—102 (114, 126) sts.
Row 4: P1, ssp, p7, *p2tog twice, [yo, p1] 4 times, p2tog twice; rep from * to last 8 sts, p5, p2tog, p1—100 (112, 124) sts.
Rows 5 and 6: P1, ssp, purl to last 3 sts, p2tog, p1—96 (108, 120) sts.
Row 7: K1, ssk, k3, *k2tog twice, [yo, k1] 4 times, k2tog twice; rep from * to last 6 sts, k3, k2tog, k1—94 (106, 118) sts.
Rows 8 and 9: K1, ssk, knit to last 3 sts, k2tog, k1—90 (102, 114) sts.
Row 10: P1, ssp, p1, *p2tog twice, [yo, p1] 4 times, p2tog twice; rep from * to last 2 sts, p2tog—88 (100, 112) sts.
Rows 11 and 12: P1, ssp, purl to last 3 sts, p2tog, p1—84 (96, 108) sts.
Bind off all sts loosely.

I-CORD EDGING
With smaller dpn, cast on 3 sts, then with same dpn, pick up (but do not knit) 1 st from bottom left sleeve edge where bottom edging meets the sleeve (at beg of the bound-off sleeve sts)—4 sts on needle. Slide sts to other end of dpn.
Work 3-st Attached I-cord until edging meets right sleeve.
Weave in ends and block. ●

SOPHIE'S SHRUG **SCHEMATIC**

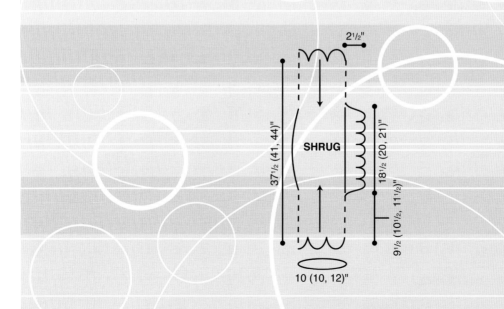

2¹/₂"

37¹/₂ (41, 44)"

SHRUG

18¹/₂ (20, 21)"

9¹/₂ (10¹/₂, 11¹/₂)"

10 (10, 12)"

LIZZIE**cropped**CARDI

DESIGN BY DIANE ZANGL

This sassy striped bolero is the perfect covering for a cool spring evening.

INTERMEDIATE

SIZES
Woman's small (medium, large, extra-large)
Instructions are given for smallest size, with larger sizes in parentheses. When only 1 number is given, it applies to all sizes.

FINISHED MEASUREMENTS
Chest: 36 (40, 44, 48) inches
Length: 17 (17½, 19½, 19½) inches

MATERIALS
Berroco Mica (worsted weight; 31% cotton/26% silk/23% nylon/20% linen; 108 yds/40g per hank):
6 (7, 8, 9) hanks mother of pearl #1102 (MC), 2 hanks each abalone #1112 (A), jarosite #1126 (B) and mushroom #1103 (C)
Size 5 (3.75mm) 29- and 36-inch circular needles or size needed to obtain gauge
Stitch holders
Stitch markers

GAUGE
24 sts and 30 rows = 4 inches/10cm in K6, P2 Rib.
To save time, take time to check gauge.

PATTERN STITCHES
K2, P2 Twisted Rib (multiple of 4 sts + 2)
Row 1 (WS): P2-tbl, *k2, p2-tbl; rep from * across.
Row 2 (RS): K2-tbl, *p2, k2-tbl; rep from * across.
Rep Rows 1 and 2 for pat.
K6, P2 Rib (multiple of 6 sts + 2)
Row 1 (WS): K2, *p6, k2; rep from * across.
Row 2 (RS): P2, *k6, p2; rep from * across.
Rep Rows 1 and 2 for pat.
Color stripe sequence
Working in K6, P2 Rib, work *10 rows MC,

6 rows A, 10 rows MC, 6 rows B, 10 rows MC, 6 rows B; rep from *.

PATTERN NOTES
This cardigan is worked in 2 pieces, which begin at the cuffs and end at the center back.
Row gauge should be accurate for proper fit.
Do not cut main color (MC) after each stripe; carry yarn along edge of contrasting color (CC) stripe, catching it every other row.
Tip: To aid in picking up stitches evenly around edge for ribbed band, place markers on each half at beginning of neck shaping, at beginning of lower edge shaping and at side seams.

RIGHT HALF
SLEEVE
With MC, cast on 74 (82, 90, 90) sts.
Work even in K2, P2 Twisted Rib for 1 inch, ending with a WS row; inc 8 sts evenly across on last row—82 (90, 98, 98) sts.
Change to K6, P2 Rib and Color Stripe sequence and work even until piece measures 5 (5, 6, 6) inches, ending with a WS row.

BODY
Cast on 56 (56, 64, 64) sts at end of next 2 rows—194 (202, 226, 226) sts.

Working new sts into established pat, work even until body measures 5¼ (6, 6¾, 7½) inches from cast-on body sts, ending with a WS row.

BACK NECK

Next row (RS): Work 103 (107, 119, 119) front sts and place on holder, work to end of row.

Work even on rem 91 (95, 107, 107) sts until body measures 9 (10, 11, 12) inches above cast-on body sts, ending with a WS row.

Place sts on holder.

FRONT NECK

Slip front sts from holder to needle.

With WS facing, join yarn at neck edge.

Bind off 12 sts, work to end of row—91 (95, 107, 107) sts.

Bind off 4 sts at neck edge 9 times—55 (59, 71, 71) sts.

Dec 1 st at neck [every row] 2 (4, 6, 8) times, and *at the same time*, when front is 16 rows short of back above cast-on body sts, dec 1 st at lower edge [every row] 8 times—45 (47, 57, 55) sts.

Bind off.

LEFT HALF

Work as for right half until piece measures 5¼ (6, 6¾, 7½) inches above cast-on body sts, ending with a WS row.

BACK NECK

Next row (RS): Work 91 (95, 107, 107) back sts, place rem 103 (107, 119, 119) front sts on holder.

Work even until back measures same as for right half.

Place sts on holder.

SHAPE FRONT NECK

Slip front sts from holder to needle.

With RS facing, join yarn at neck edge; work 2 rows even.

Next row (RS): Bind off 12 sts, work to end of row—91 (95, 107, 107) sts.

Bind off 4 sts at neck edge 9 times—55 (59, 71, 71) sts.

Dec 1 st at neck [every row] 2 (4, 6, 8) times, and *at the same time*, when front is 16 rows short of back above cast-on body sts, dec 1 st at lower edge every row 8 times—45 (47, 57, 55) sts.

Bind off.

FINISHING

Weave in all ends; block pieces to finished measurements.

Graft center back seam, using Kitchener st.

Sew sleeve and side seams.

RIBBED EDGING

With longer needle and MC, beg at center back neck, pick up and knit 1 st in each st, and 3 sts for every 4 rows around entire body, matching st counts for each side; adjust st count, if necessary, to equal a multiple of 4. Place marker for beg of rnd and join.

Ribbing rnd: K1-tbl, *p2, k2-tbl; rep from * to last 3 sts, p2, k1-tbl.

Rep Ribbing rnd 4 times more.

Bind off loosely in rib. ●

LIZZIE CROPPED CARDI **SCHEMATIC**

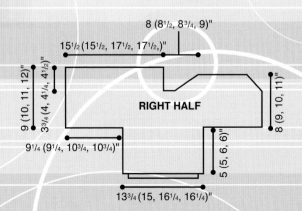

KID'S cuff-to-cuff TOP

DESIGN BY KYLEANN WILLIAMS

This easy knit and purl pullover is a timeless classic.

 EASY

SIZES
Child's 2 (4, 6, 8) Instructions are given for smallest size, with larger sizes in parentheses. When only one number is given, it applies to all sizes.

FINISHED MEASUREMENTS
Chest: 25 (26½, 29, 30½) inches
Length: 12 (14½, 15¾, 17½) inches

MATERIALS
Crystal Palace Bamboozle (worsted weight; 55% bamboo/24% cotton/21% elastic nylon; 90 yds/50g per ball): 6 (7, 8, 9) balls pink print #2005
Size 9 (5.5mm) 16- and 24-inch circular needles or size needed to obtain gauge

4 MEDIUM

GAUGE
20 sts and 28 rows = 4 inches/10cm in Welted Stripes pat.
To save time, take time to check gauge.

SPECIAL ABBREVIATIONS
Increase 1 (inc1): Increase by knitting or purling in front and back of st, depending on pat row.
Decrease 1 (dec1): Decrease in pat as follows: if on a knit row, ssk at right edge and k2tog at left edge; if on a purl row, ssp at right edge and p2tog at left edge.

PATTERN STITCH
Welted Stripes (any number of sts)
Rows 1 and 3 (RS): Knit.
Rows 2 and 4: Purl.
Rows 5 and 7: Purl.
Rows 6 and 8: Knit.
    Rep Rows 1–8 for pat.

PATTERN NOTES
This sweater is worked from cuff to cuff.
    Work selvedge stitches in pattern, knit on knit rows and purl on purl rows.

LEFT SLEEVE
With longer needle, cast on 29 (31, 33, 35) sts.
    Work K1, P1 Rib for 1½ (2, 2, 2) inches, ending with a WS row and inc 3 (3, 5, 5) sts evenly across last row—32 (34, 38, 40) sts.
    Change to Welted Stripes pat.
Inc row (RS): Work 1 selvedge st (see Pattern Notes), inc1, work to last 2 sts, inc1, work 1 selvedge st.
    Maintaining pat, rep Inc row [every 2 rows] 1 (0, 0, 0) time(s), [every 4 rows] 7 (10, 12, 10) times, and [every 6 rows] 0 (1, 1, 4) time(s)—50 (60, 66, 70) sts.
    Work even until piece measures 7 (9, 10, 12½) inches, ending with a WS row.

BODY
Turn work and using cable method, cast on 28 (32, 36, 42) sts for back.
Next row (RS): Continuing in established pat, work across cast-on sts, work 25 (30, 33, 35) sleeve sts, place marker for shoulder line, work rem sleeve sts; turn work and using cable method, cast on 28 (32, 36, 42) sts for front—106 (124, 138, 154) sts.
    Work even for 3¼ (3¼, 3¾, 4) inches, ending with a WS row.

Shape left front neck
Next row (RS): Work to marker and remove it; attach 2nd ball, bind off 1 st, work to end of row—52 (61, 68, 76) front sts.
    Continue working front and back simultaneously with 2 separate balls of yarn.
Dec row (WS): Front: work to 2 sts before front neck edge, dec1; back: work even—51 (60, 67, 75) front sts.

Bind-off row (RS): Back: work even; front: bind off 2 (2, 1, 1) st work to end—49 (58, 66, 74) front sts.

Sizes 2 and 4 only
Rep last 2 rows once—46 (55) front sts.

Size 6 only
Rep last 2 rows once, then rep Dec row once more—62 front sts.

Size 8 only
Next row: Rep Dec row—73 front sts.
Bind-off row (RS): Work back even; bind off 2 sts, work to end—71 front sts.

Rep last 2 rows once—68 front sts.

All sizes
Work 31 (37, 36, 37) rows even, ending on a WS row.

Shape right front neck
Cast-on row (RS): Back: work even; front: cast on 2 (2, 1, 2) sts at neck edge, work to end—48 (57, 63, 70) front sts.
Inc row: Work to 2 sts before neck edge, inc1, work 1; work back even—49 (58, 64, 71) front sts.

Sizes 2 and 4 only
Rep last 2 rows once—52 (61) sts.

Size 6 only
Rep last 2 rows once, then work Cast-on row once more—68 sts.

Size 8 only
Rep last 2 rows once—74 sts.

Next 2 rows: Working in established pat, inc1 at front neck edge—76 sts.

All sizes
Next row: Working with 1 ball of yarn only, work across all sts and inc1 at neck edge—53 (62, 69, 77) front sts; 106 (124, 138, 154) sts total.

Work even for 3¼ (3¼, 3¾, 4) inches, ending with a WS row.

SECOND SLEEVE

Next 2 rows: Bind off 28 (32, 36, 42) sts, work to end—50 (60, 66, 70) sleeve sts rem.

Work 4 (0, 0, 0) rows even.

Dec row (RS): Maintaining pat, work 1 selvedge st, dec1, work to last 3 sts, dec1, work 1 selvedge st—48 (58, 64, 68) sts.

Continuing in established pat, rep Dec row [every 6 rows] 0 (0, 0, 3) times, [every 4 rows]

6 (11, 13, 11) times, and [every 2 rows] 2 (0, 0, 0) times—32 (36, 38, 40) sts.

Work even until sleeve measures 5½ (7, 8, 10½) inches, ending with a WS row and dec 3 (3, 5, 5) sts across last row—29 (33, 33, 35) sts.

Work in K1, P1 Rib for 1½ (2, 2, 2) inches.
Bind off in rib.

FINISHING

Weave in ends and block.
Sew side and sleeve seams.

BOTTOM BAND

Pick up and knit approx 120 (126, 140, 146) sts evenly around bottom of sweater.

Work in K1, P1 Rib for 1½ (2, 2, 2) inches.
Bind off loosely in rib.

NECK BAND

With RS facing and using shorter needle, pick up and knit 70 (76, 78, 80) sts evenly around neck edge.

Work K1, P1 Rib for 1 inch.
Bind off very loosely in rib. ●

KID'S CUFF-TO-CUFF TOP **SCHEMATIC**

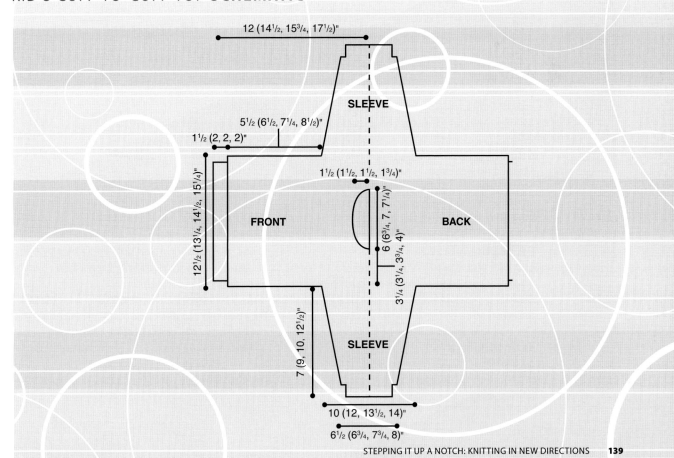

LITTLE**bit**O'**sugar**

DESIGN BY ELLEN EDWARDS DRECHSLER

Sugar and spice and everything nice!

 INTERMEDIATE

SIZES
Girl's 2 (4, 6, 8) Instructions are given for smallest size, with larger sizes in parentheses. When only 1 number is given, it applies to all sizes.

FINISHED MEASUREMENTS
Chest: 20¼ (23¼, 25, 27¼) inches
Length: 14 (17, 18¼, 19¼) inches

MATERIALS
Plymouth Happy Feet DK (DK weight; 90% superwash merino wool/10% nylon; 262 yds/100g per skein): 3 (3, 4, 4) skeins green/yellow #56
Size 6 (4mm) 24-inch circular needle or size needed to obtain gauge
Size 4 (3.5mm) 16-inch circular needle
Stitch marker

GAUGE
22 sts and 28 rows/rnds = 4 inches/10cm in St st with larger needle.
To save time, take time to check gauge.

SPECIAL ABBREVIATION
Make 1 (M1): Insert LH needle from front to back under the running thread between the last st worked and next st on RH needle; knit into the back of resulting loop.

PATTERN NOTE
This dress is worked in 2 parts. The sleeves and yoke are worked in 1 piece from cuff to cuff; the body is picked up along the edge of the top and worked in the round down to the edge.

TOP SECTION
SLEEVE
With larger needle, cast on 40 (68, 78, 80) sts; do not join.

Knit 16 rows.
Change to St st and work even until piece measures 11 (12, 14, 15½) inches, ending with a WS row.

YOKE
Cast on 10 sts at beg of next 2 rows—60 (88, 98, 100) sts.
Work even for 1½ (2, 2, 2½) inches, ending with a WS row.

NECK
K29 (43, 48, 49), join 2nd ball of yarn and bind off 2 sts, knit to end—29 (43, 48, 49) sts each side.
Working both sides simultaneously, work even until neck opening measures 7½ (8, 9, 9) inches, ending with a WS row.
Next row (RS): Using 1 ball of yarn, knit to neck opening, cast on 2 sts, knit to end of row; cut 2nd ball of yarn—60 (88, 98, 100) sts.
Work even for 1½ (2, 2, 2½) inches, ending with a WS row.
Bind off 10 sts at beg of next 2 rows—40 (68, 78, 80) sts.

SLEEVE
Work even until sleeve measures same as first sleeve to garter ridges.
Knit 16 rows.
Bind off.
Sew side and underarm seams.

BODY
With RS facing and using larger needle, beg at a side seam, pick up and knit 112 (128, 138, 150) sts evenly around; place marker for beg of rnd and join.
Work even in St st for 1½ (2, 1½, 1) inch(es).
Inc rnd: Using M1 inc, inc 13 (11, 15, 12) sts evenly around—125 (139, 153, 162) sts.
Work even until lower body measures 3½ (2½, 2½, 2) inches.
Inc rnd: Using M1 inc, inc 13 (11, 15, 12) sts evenly around—138 (150, 168, 174) sts.

Work even until body measures approx 8¼ (8¾, 9¼, 9¾) inches or desired length.
[Knit 1 rnd, purl 1 rnd] twice.
Bind off very loosely.

FINISHING
Neck edging
With RS facing and using smaller needle, pick up and knit 98 (104, 118, 118) sts evenly around neck edge; place marker and join.
Beg with a purl rnd, work 5 rnds in garter st.
Bind off very loosely kwise, using larger needle if necessary.
Weave in all ends. Block to finished measurements. ●

LITTLE BIT O' SUGAR SCHEMATICS

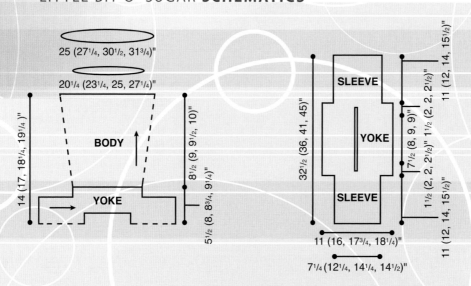

25 (27¼, 30½, 31¾)"

20¼ (23¼, 25, 27¼)"

BODY

14 (17, 18¼, 19¼)"

8½ (9, 9½, 10)"

YOKE

5½ (8, 8¾, 9¼)"

SLEEVE

YOKE

SLEEVE

32½ (36, 41, 45)"

11 (12, 14, 15½)"

7½ (8, 9, 9)"

1½ (2, 2, 2½)"

1½ (2, 2, 2½)"

11 (12, 14, 15½)"

11 (16, 17¾, 18¼)"

7¼ (12¼, 14¼, 14½)"

CHAIN-LINK**cardigan**

DESIGN BY AMY POLCYN

Strut your stuff when you wear this glamorous cardigan with eye-catching chain-link accents.

■■■□ INTERMEDIATE

SIZES
Woman's small (medium, large, extra-large, 2X-large) Instructions are given for smallest size, with larger sizes in parentheses. When only 1 number is given, it applies to all sizes.

FINISHED MEASUREMENTS
Body Chest: 36 (40, 44, 48, 52) inches
Length: 20¼ (21½, 22¼, 23½, 24¾) inches

MATERIALS
Berroco Comfort DK (DK weight; 50% super fine nylon/50% super fine acrylic; 178 yds/50g per ball): 6 (6, 7, 7, 8) balls crypto crystalline #2758 (MC), 1 ball Aegean Sea #2753 (CC1), 1 ball boy blue #2707 (CC2)
Size 6 (4mm) 32-inch circular needle or size needed to obtain gauge

3 LIGHT

GAUGE
24 sts and 32 rows = 4 inches/10cm in St st.
To save time, take time to check gauge.

PATTERN STITCH
Chain pat (multiple of 8 sts + 6)
Row 1 (RS): With CC1, knit.
Row 2: With CC1, knit.
Row 3: With MC,*k6, sl 2; rep from * to last 6 sts, k6.
Row 4: With MC, p6, *sl 2, p6; rep from * to end.
Row 5: With CC1, rep Row 3.
Row 6: With CC1, knit.
Row 7: With MC, knit.
Row 8: With MC, purl.
Rows 9 and 10: With CC2, rep Rows 1 and 2.
Row 11: With MC, *k2, sl 2, k4; rep from * to last 6 sts, k2, sl 2, k2.

Row 12: With MC, p2, *sl 2, p6; rep from * to last 4 sts, sl 1, p2.
Row 13: With CC2, rep Row 11.
Row 14: With CC2, knit.
Rows 15 and 16: With MC, rep Rows 7 and 8.

PATTERN NOTES
Jacket is worked in one piece from cuff to cuff.
When working Chain pattern on body, use

intarsia method (see page 170) for working garter border with Main Color (MC).

SLEEVE

With MC, cast on 62 (70, 70, 78, 78) sts.

Work in garter st for 1 inch.

Change to St st and work 6 rows.

Work Rows 1–16 of Chain pat, then Rows 1–6 once more.

With MC, continue in St st and inc 1 st each end [every 4 rows] 18 (18, 18, 18, 22) times—98 (106, 106, 114, 122) sts.

Work even until sleeve measures 17 (17½, 18, 18½, 19) inches, ending with a WS row.

BODY

Cast on 72 (76, 80, 84, 88) sts at beg of next 2 rows—242 (258, 266, 282, 298) sts.

Next 18 rows: Work first and last 6 sts in garter st for border and rem sts in St st.

Next 22 rows: Maintaining first and last 6 border sts in garter st with MC, work rem sts in Chain pat.

Work even with MC, maintaining 6-st garter borders and rem sts in St st until body measures 5 (6, 6¾, 7¾, 8½) inches, ending with a WS row.

Work 1 inch more with first 126 (134, 138, 148, 156) sts (front band) and last 6 sts in garter st, ending with a WS row.

Next row (RS): Bind off 120 (128, 132, 142, 150) front sts, work in established pat to end for back.

Maintaining first and last 6 sts in garter st, work even for 6 (6, 6½, 6½, 7) inches for back neck, ending with a WS row.

Next row (RS): Cast on 120 (128, 132, 142, 150) sts, work in pat to end.

Keeping first 126 (134, 138, 148, 156) sts and last 6 sts in garter st, work even for 1 inch, ending with a WS row.

Work first and last 6 sts in garter st and rem sts in St st until piece measures same as other Front from edge to beg of Chain pat, ending with a WS row.

Work 22 rows Chain pat.

Work even in St st until 2nd front measures same as first front.

Bind off 72 (76, 80, 84, 88) sts at beg of next 2 rows—98 (106, 106, 114, 122) sts.

SLEEVE

Working in St st, dec 1 st each end [every 4 rows] 18 (18, 18, 18, 22) times—62 (70, 70, 78, 78) sts.

Work even until 2nd sleeve measures same as first sleeve to Chain pat.

Work 22 rows Chain pat.

Work 6 rows in St st.

Work in garter st for 1 inch.

Bind off.

FINISHING

Weave in ends. Block to finished measurements.

Sew side and sleeve seams. ●

CHAIN-LINK CARDIGAN **SCHEMATIC & CHART**

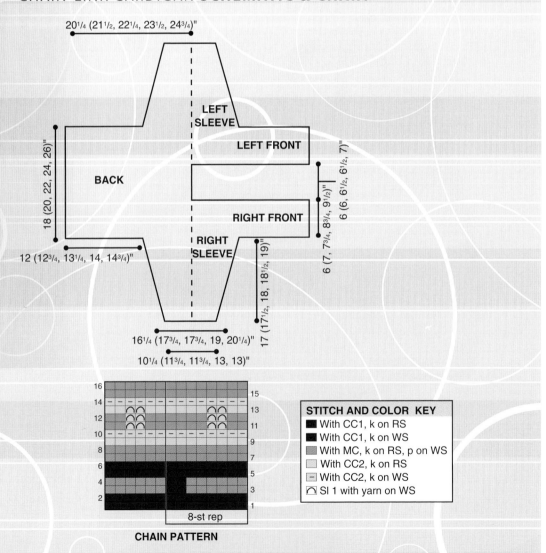

CHAIN PATTERN

8-st rep

STITCH AND COLOR KEY
- ■ With CC1, k on RS
- ■ With CC1, k on WS
- ▨ With MC, k on RS, p on WS
- □ With CC2, k on RS
- – With CC2, k on WS
- ⌒ Sl 1 with yarn on WS

20¼ (21½, 22¼, 23½, 24¾)"

18 (20, 22, 24, 26)"

12 (12¾, 13¼, 14, 14¾)"

LEFT SLEEVE

LEFT FRONT

BACK

RIGHT FRONT

RIGHT SLEEVE

6 (6, 6½, 6½, 7)"

6 (7, 7¾, 8¾, 9½)"

17 (17½, 18, 18½, 19)"

16¼ (17¾, 17¾, 19, 20¼)"

10¼ (11¾, 11¾, 13, 13)"

CASUAL**side-to-side**VEST

DESIGN BY ANDRA KNIGHT-BOWMAN

Hate to deal with those loose ends? This vest is a sure hit with minimal sewing.

 EASY

SIZES
Woman's small (medium, large, extra-large, 2X-large) Instructions are given for smallest size, with larger sizes in parentheses. When only 1 number is given, it applies to all sizes.

FINISHED MEASUREMENTS
Chest (with collar folded back): 38 (42, 46, 50, 54) inches
Length to shoulder: 21 (22, 23, 24, 25) inches

MATERIALS
Nashua Handknits Vignette (bulky weight; 100% superwash wool; 93 yds/50g per skein): 9 (11, 13, 14, 16) skeins dusk #NVIG.0012
Size 11 (8mm) 24-inch circular needle or size needed to obtain gauge
Size L/11 (8mm) crochet hook

GAUGE
13 sts and 28 rows = 4 inches/10cm in garter st. To save time, take time to check gauge.

SPECIAL TECHNIQUE
Crochet Cast-On: Make slip knot on crochet hook. *Hold crochet hook vertically in front of and at right angle to the needle with the needle point facing right. Take the yarn under the needle, up and across the front of the crochet hook. Pull yarn through loop—new st on needle. Rep from * as required. Slip loop from crochet hook to needle to form the last st.

PATTERN NOTES
This vest is made sideways in one piece. If you want your vest to be shorter/longer, cast on fewer/more stitches (approximately 3 stitches

per inch) and then follow pattern.
Slip first stitch of every row purlwise with yarn in front.

RIGHT FRONT COLLAR
Using crochet method, cast on 80 (85, 89, 91, 96) sts.
Row 1 (RS): Sl 1 wyif, bring yarn to back and knit to end.
Slipping first st of every row, continue in garter st until work measures 4½ (5, 5½, 6, 6 ½) inches, ending with a WS row.
Next row (RS): Bind off 11 (13, 15, 13, 15) sts, knit to end—69 (72, 74, 78, 81) sts.

RIGHT FRONT
Work even for 4 (4½, 5, 5½, 6) inches, ending with a WS row.

Underarm

Next row (RS): Bind off 22 (24, 26, 28, 30) sts, knit to end—47 (48, 48, 50, 51) sts.

Work even for 4 (4, 4, 6, 6) inches, ending with a WS row.

BACK

Next row (RS): Cast on 22 (24, 26, 28, 30) sts at beg of row, then knit across—69 (72, 74, 78, 81) sts.

Work even for 15 (17, 19, 19, 21) inches, ending with a WS row.

Underarm

Next row (RS): Bind off 22 (24, 26, 28, 30) sts, knit to end—47 (48, 48, 50, 51) sts

Work even for 4 (4, 4, 6, 6) inches, ending with a WS row.

LEFT FRONT

Next row (RS): Cast on 22 (24, 26, 28, 30) sts, knit across—69 (72, 74, 78, 81) sts.

Work even for 4 (4½, 5, 5½, 6) inches, ending with a WS row.

LEFT FRONT COLLAR

Next row (RS): Cast on 11 (13, 15, 13, 15) sts, knit across—80 (85, 89, 91, 96) sts.

Work even for 4½ (5, 5½, 6, 6½) inches, ending with a WS row.

Bind off loosely.

FINISHING

Weave in ends. Block to finished measurements.

Sew shoulder seams. Sew tops of left and right collars tog. Sew sides of collar to back neck. ●

CASUAL SIDE-TO-SIDE VEST **SCHEMATIC**

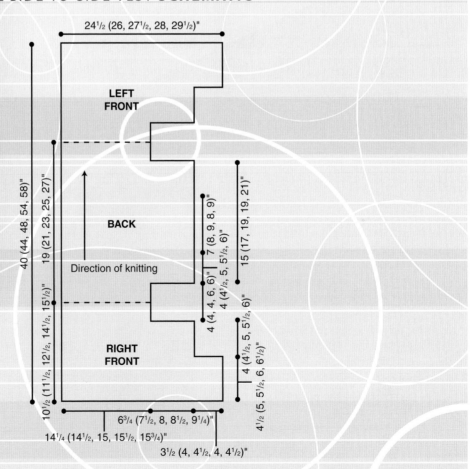

CELTICvineHAT&FINGERLESSgloves

DESIGNS BY DIANE ZANGL

Fingerless gloves, along with a matching hat, show off a unique vine and leaf pattern.

■■■■ EXPERIENCED

SIZES
Hat: One size fits most
Gloves: Small/medium (medium/large)
Instructions are given for both sizes, with larger size in parentheses. When only 1 number is given, it applies to both sizes.

FINISHED MEASUREMENTS
Hat circumference: Approx 20 inches
Glove length: 5½ (6) inches
Palm circumference: 8 (9) inches

MATERIALS
Classic Elite Inca Alpaca (DK weight; 100% alpaca; 109 yds/ 50g per hank): 3 hanks damask red #1153

(3 LIGHT)

Size 3 (3.25mm) double-point and 16-inch circular needles or size needed to obtain gauge
Size D/3 (3.25mm) crochet hook
Cable needle
Stitch markers, 1 in CC for beg of rnd

GAUGE
22 sts and 32 rnds = 4 inches/10cm in St st.
25-st Leaf panel = 3½ inches/9cm.
To save time, take time to check gauge.

SPECIAL ABBREVIATIONS
Place marker (pm): Place a marker on needle to separate sections.
Slip marker (sm): Slip marker as you come to it.
Make 1 (M1): Make a backwards loop and place on RH needle.
N1, N2, N3: Needle 1, Needle 2, Needle 3

PATTERN STITCH
See chart.
For hat, read all odd-numbered (RS) rows of chart from right to left; read even-numbered rows (WS) from left to right.
For gloves, read all rnds of chart from right to left.
Use Rnds 1-28 of chart for right glove and Rnds 29-56 for left glove.

SPECIAL TECHNIQUE
Provisional Cast-On: With crochet hook and waste yarn, make a chain several sts longer than desired cast-on. With knitting needle and project yarn, pick up indicated number of sts in the "bumps" on back of chain. When indicated in pattern, "unzip" the crochet chain to free live sts.

PATTERN NOTES
The hat begins with a long band which is worked back and forth; stitches are picked up along a long edge to form the crown; the picot-hemmed lower edge is worked in the same manner.

Bind off all fingers very loosely, using a larger needle if necessary.

HAT

SIDES
Using provisional method, cast on 49 sts.
Set up pat (WS): P12, pm, k13, p3, k9, pm, p12.
Keeping 25 sts between markers in chart pat and all others in St st, work 3 complete reps of chart.
Cut yarn leaving a long end.
Unzip provisional cast-on, placing sts on a spare needle.
Graft edges using Kitchener st.

PICOT BORDER
Pick up and knit 112 sts (approx 2 sts for every 3 rows) along one long edge of hat; pm and join. Knit 3 rnds.
Turning rnd: *Yo, k2tog; rep from * around.

Knit 4 rnds.

Bind off very loosely.

Turn hem to inside of hat and sew in place.

CROWN

Pick up and knit 112 sts around opposite long edge of hat.

Knit 2 rnds.

Dec rnd: K2tog around—56 sts.

Rep [last 3 rnds] 3 times more, changing to dpns when necessary—7 sts.

Cut yarn, leaving a 6-inch tail.

Using tapestry needle, thread tail through rem sts twice, and pull tight.

FINISHING

Weave in all ends. Block.

GLOVES

RIGHT GLOVE
CUFF

With dpns, cast on 48 (54) sts; pm for beg of rnd and join, taking care not to twist sts.

Work K1, P1 Rib for 1½ inches and inc 2 sts on last rnd—49 (55) sts.

Rearrange sts so there are 25 sts on N1, and 12 (15) sts each on N2 and N3.

Size medium/large only

Next 3 rnds: N1: Work Rnd 28 of chart; N2 and N3: knit.

THUMB GUSSET

Rnd 1 (set-up): N1: work Rnd 1 of chart; N2: k1, pm, p1, k3, p1, pm, knit to end; N3: knit.

Continue to work chart pat on N1 and St st on N3, forming thumb gusset on N2 as follows:

Rnd 2: N2: k1, sm, p1, k3, p1, sm, knit to end.

Rnd 3: N2: k1, sm, p1, M1, knit to purl st, M1, p1, sm, knit to end.

Rnds 4 and 5: N2: k1, sm, p1, knit to purl st, p1, sm, knit to end.

Rep [Rnds 3–5] 4 times more—15 sts between markers.

Rnd 18: N2: k2, slip next 13 sts to waste yarn, cast on 3 sts, knit to end.

Work even, working chart pat on N1 and St st on N2 and N3, until Rnd 28 of chart has been completed.

FINGER OPENINGS
Pinkie

Rnd 1: [K1, p1] 3 times, slip rem 19 sts of N1, all sts of N2, and 6 (8) sts of N3 to waste yarn, *k1, p1; rep from * to last 0 (3) sts, k1, p2tog—12 sts.

Divide sts onto 3 needles.

Work 2 rnds in K1, P1 Rib.

Bind off in rib.

Ring finger

Rnd 1: Pick up and knit 2 sts at base of pinkie, work all sts from waste yarn as they present themselves.

Rnd 2: [K1, p1] 4 times, slip next 25 (28) sts back to waste yarn, [k1, p1] 3 (4) times—14 (16) sts.

Complete as for pinkie.

Middle finger

Rnd 1: Pick up and knit 2 sts at base of ring finger, work 6 sts from back of hand as they present themselves, leave next 13 (14) sts on waste yarn, k6 (8) palm sts—14 (16) sts.

Work 3 rnds in K1, P1 Rib.

Bind off in rib.

Index finger

Rnd 1: Pick up and knit 2 sts at base of middle finger, work rem sts as they present themselves—14 (16) sts.

Work 3 rnds in K1, P1 Rib.

Bind off in rib.

Thumb

Slip sts from waste yarn to 2 dpns, with 7 sts on N1 and 6 on N2; with N3, join yarn and pick up and knit 6 sts at top of thumb opening.

Rnd 1: [K1, p1] twice, k1, p2tog, [k1, p1] to end of rnd—18 sts.

Work 2 rnds in K1, P1 Rib.

Bind off in rib.

LEFT GLOVE
CUFF

Cast on and work lower ribbing as for right glove—49 (55) sts.

Rearrange sts so there are 12 (15) sts each on N1 and N2 and 25 sts on N3.

Size medium/large only

Next 3 rnds: N1 and N2: knit; N3: work Rnd 56 of chart.

Thumb gusset

Rnd 1 (set-up): N1: knit; N2: knit to last 6 sts, pm, p1, k3, p1, pm, k1; N3: work chart, beg with Rnd 29.

Work in established pats until chart is

complete, working thumb gusset between markers on N2 as for right glove.

Work even, working St st and N1 and N2 and chart pat on N3, until Rnd 56 of chart has been completed.

FINGER OPENINGS
Pinkie
Rnd 1: [K1, p1] 3 times, slip rem sts of N1, all sts of N2 and 19 sts of N2 to waste yarn; *k1, p1; rep from * to last 0 (3) sts, k1, p2tog—12 sts.

Divide sts onto 3 needles.
Work 2 rnds in K1, P1 Rib.
Bind off in rib.

Ring finger
Rnd 1: Pick up and knit 2 sts at base of pinkie, work all sts from waste yarn as they present themselves.
Rnd 2: [K1, p1] 4 (5) times, slip next 25 (28) sts

back to waste yarn, [k1, p1] 3 times—14 (16) sts.
Complete as for pinkie.

Middle finger
Rnd 1: Pick up and knit 2 sts at base of ring finger, knit next 6 (8) palm sts, leaving next 13 (14) sts on waste yarn, work 6 back hand sts as they present themselves—14 (16) sts.
Work 3 rnds in K1, P1 Rib.
Bind off in rib.

Index finger
Work as for right glove.

Thumb
Work as for right glove.

FINISHING
Weave in ends, using them to close holes between fingers if necessary.
Block. ●

CELTIC VINE HAT & FINGERLESS GLOVES **CHART & STITCH KEY**

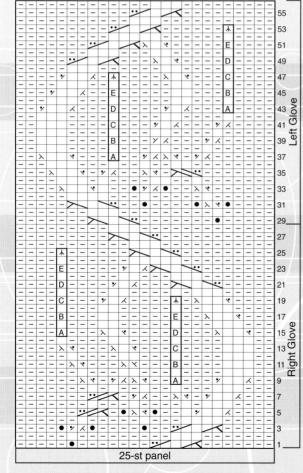

CHART

25-st panel

Left Glove

Right Glove

STITCH KEY
- ☐ K on RS, p on WS.
- − P on RS, k on WS.
- ● Bobble: (K1, yo, k1) in same st, turn; p3, turn; k3, turn; p3, turn; sl 2 sts tog kwise, k1, p2sso.
- Sl 1 to cn and hold in back, k1, k1 from cn.
- Sl 1 to cn and hold in front, k1, k1 from cn.
- Sl 1 to cn and hold back, k1, p1 from cn.
- Sl 1 to cn and hold in front, p1, k1 from cn.
- Sl 2 to cn and hold in back, k1, p2 from cn.
- Sl 1 to cn and hold in front, p2, k1 from cn.
- Sl 1 to cn and hold in back, k3, p1 from cn.
- Sl 3 to cn and hold in front, p1, k3 from cn.
- Sl 2 to cn and hold in back, k3, p2 from cn.
- Sl 3 to cn and hold in front, p2, k3 from cn.
- ⋏ LEAF: Work all even-number rows/rnds in St st; st count will vary on each row.
  - A: [K1, yo, k1, yo, k1] in same st—5 sts.
  - B: Over 5 previous sts, work: k2, yo, k1, yo, k2—7 sts.
  - C: K7.
  - D: Ssk, k3, k2tog—5 sts.
  - E: Ssk, k1, k2tog—3 sts.
  - ⋏ Sl 2 sts tog kwise, k1, p2sso.

JUSTtheRIGHTjacket

DESIGN BY PAULINE SCHULTZ

The fashion-forward design, along with impressive shaping details, makes this piece a must for your wardrobe.

 EASY

SIZES
Woman's small (medium, large, extra-large, 2X-large, 3X-large, 4X-large) Instructions are given for smallest size, with larger sizes in parentheses. When only 1 number is given, it applies to all sizes.

FINISHED MEASUREMENTS
Chest: 36 (40, 44, 48, 52, 56, 60) inches
Length: 20½ (20¾, 20¾, 21, 21, 21¼, 21¼) inches

MATERIALS
ShiBuiKnits Merino Kid (DK weight; 55% kid mohair/45% merino wool; 218 yds/100g per skein): 6 (7, 8, 8, 9, 10, 11) skeins honey #MK1395
Crochet cotton (waste yarn)
Size 3 (3.25mm) 24- or 36-inch circular needle or size needed to obtain gauge
2 size 6 (4mm) 24- or 36-inch circular needles or size needed to obtain gauge
Size G/6 (4mm) crochet hook
Stitch markers

GAUGE
26 sts and 34 rows = 4 inches/10cm in K1, P1 rib on smaller needle.
21 sts and 38 rows = 4 inches/10cm in Basket Weave pat on larger needles (washed and blocked).
To save time, take time to check gauge.

SPECIAL TECHNIQUES
Crochet Cast-On: Make slip knot on crochet hook. *Hold crochet hook vertically in front of and at right angles to the needle with the needle point facing right. Take the yarn under the needle, up and across the front of the crochet hook. Pull yarn through loop—new st on needle. Rep from * as required. Slip loop from crochet hook to needle to form the last st.
Provisional Cast-On: With crochet hook and waste yarn, make a chain several sts longer than desired cast-on. With knitting needle and project yarn, pick up indicated number of sts in the "bumps" on back of chain. When indicated in pattern, "unzip" the crochet chain to free live sts.
3-Needle Bind-Off: With RS tog and needles parallel, using a 3rd needle, knit tog a st from the front needle with 1 from the back. *Knit tog a st from the front and back needles, and slip the first st over the 2nd to bind off. Rep from * across, then fasten off last st.

PATTERN STITCH
Basket Weave (multiple of 6 sts + 8)
Row 1 and all RS rows: Knit.
Rows 2 and 4: P2, *k4, p2; rep from * end.
Rows 6 and 8: K3, *p2, k4; rep from * to last 5 sts, p2, k3.
Rep Rows 1–8 for pat.

PATTERN NOTES

This jacket is worked from in 1 piece cuff to cuff. The lower edge of the body is worked in garter stitch and side seams are joined using 3-Needle Bind-Off. The shawl collar is worked after the main sweater is complete.

To maximize the subtle color changes of hand-painted yarn and avoid slight differences between skeins, work with two skeins at once, alternating strands every 2 rows. When working the ribbed sleeves, change strands at the edge; when working the body, change strands at the top shoulder as this will help to reinforce the shoulder and back neck; when working the collar, change strands at the center back on the right side (RS) of garment (collar will fold back, hiding the strand change).

SLEEVE

With smaller needle and project yarn, using crochet method, cast on 110 (112, 112, 114, 114, 114, 114) sts.

Work in K1, P1 Rib until sleeve measures 8 (8½, 8¾, 9, 9¼, 9½, 9¾) inches or desired length, ending with a RS row.

BODY

Row 1 (WS): Change to larger needle; bind off 1 st, work in rib to end of row.

Row 2: Bind off 1 st, knit to end of row, then provisionally cast on 54 (54, 54, 54, 54, 55, 55) front sts—162 (164, 164, 166, 166, 167, 167) sts.

Row 3: K5 (6, 6, 7, 7, 8, 8), place marker, beg with Row 2 of Basket Weave pat, work across row, then provisionally cast on 54 (54, 54, 54,

54, 55, 55) back sts—216 (218, 218, 220, 220, 222, 222) sts.

Row 4: K5 (6, 6, 7, 7, 8, 8), place marker, work in pat to marker, knit to end of row.

Maintaining first and last 5 (6, 6, 7, 7, 8, 8) sts in garter st, work even until body measures 6½ (7, 8¼, 9¼, 10¼, 11, 12) inches, ending with a WS row.

Divide for back neck

Next row (RS): Work 108 (109, 109, 110, 110, 111, 111) back sts, turn and slip rem 108 (109, 109, 110, 110, 111, 111) front sts to waste yarn.

Work even on back sts for 5 (5½, 5½, 5½, 5½, 6, 6) inches, ending with a WS row.

Next row (RS): Work back sts to neck edge, then provisionally cast on 108 (109, 109, 110, 110, 111, 111) front sts, placing marker before last 5 (6, 6, 7, 7, 8, 8) sts—216 (218, 218, 220, 220, 222, 222) sts.

Work even until front measures 6½ (7, 8¼, 9¼, 10¼, 11, 12) inches, ending with a WS row.

Next row (RS): Work 162 (164, 164, 166, 166, 167, 167) sts, turn and slip rem front 54 (54, 54, 54, 54, 55, 55) front sts to waste yarn.

Next row: Work 108 (110, 110, 112, 112, 112, 112) sleeve sts, turn and slip rem 54 (54, 54, 54, 54, 55, 55) back sts to waste yarn.

SLEEVE

Next row (RS): Work in K1, P1 Rib and inc 1 st at beg and end of row—110 (112, 112, 114, 114, 114, 114) sts.

Change to smaller needle and continue in rib until sleeve measures 8 (8½, 8¾, 9, 9¼, 9½, 9¾) inches or same as first sleeve.

Bind off loosely in rib.

FINISHING

Weave in ends and block to finished measurements.

Transfer right front and back side sts to larger needle, with each set of sts at opposite ends of needle. Join using 3-Needle Bind-Off.

Rep for left side seam.

Sew sleeve seams.

COLLAR

Unzip front cast-on and transfer live sts to larger needle; transfer other front sts from waste yarn to larger needle.

With RS facing, work P1, K1 Rib across 1 set of front sts, pick up 27 (27, 29, 29, 31, 31, 33) sts in rib across back neck, continue in rib to end of row—243 (245, 247, 249, 251, 253, 255) sts.

Continue in rib for 4 (4½, 5, 6, 7, 7½, 8) inches. Bind off very loosely in rib.

Weave in rem ends. ●

JUST THE RIGHT JACKET **SCHEMATIC**

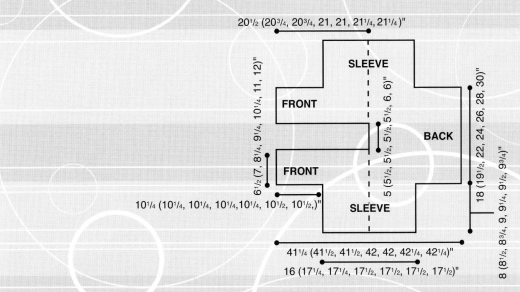

PROVENCE**pullover**

DESIGN BY DIANE ZANGL

This casual pullover with central cable detail, offers some unique and unexpected construction approaches.

INTERMEDIATE

SIZES
Woman's small (medium, large, extra-large) Instructions are given for smallest size, with larger sizes in parentheses. When only 1 number is given, it applies to all sizes.

FINISHED MEASUREMENTS
Chest: 36 (40, 44, 48) inches
Length: 22½ (23¼, 24, 25) inches

MATERIALS
Classic Elite Desert (worsted weight; 100% wool; 110 yds/50g per ball): 9 (10, 12, 13) balls copper canyon #2043
Size 7 (4.5mm) 29-inch circular needle or size needed to obtain gauge
Cable needle
Stitch markers, 1 in CC for beg of rnd
Stitch holders

4 MEDIUM

GAUGE
22 sts and 22 rows = 4 inches/10cm in K1, P1 Rib (unstretched).
17 sts and 24 rows = 4 inches/10cm in St st.
To save time, take time to check gauge.

SPECIAL ABBREVIATIONS
M1 (Make 1): Make a backwards loop and place on RH needle.
6 over 6 Left Cross (6/6 LC): Sl 6 sts to cn and hold in front, k6, k6 from cn.
Place marker (pm): Place a marker on needle to separate sections.

PATTERN STITCHES
K1, P1 Rib (odd number of sts)

Row 1 (WS): P1, *k1, p1; rep from * across.
Row 2 (RS): K1, *p1, k1; rep from * across.
Rep Rows 1 and 2 for pat.
Center Cable Panel (16-st panel)
Rnds 1–3: P2, k12, p2.
Rnd 4: P2, 6/6 LC, p2.
Rnds 5–16: Rep Rnd 1.
Rep Rnds 1–16 for pat.

PATTERN NOTE
The sleeves and yokes are worked together from side to side as single units, then the 2 pieces are joined at center front and back. Body stitches are picked up and worked down from the yoke in the round.

RIGHT SLEEVE & YOKE
Cast on 55 (61, 67, 71) sts.
Beg with a WS row, work 5 rows in K1, P1 Rib.
Inc row (RS): K1, M1, work in established rib to last st, M1, k1.

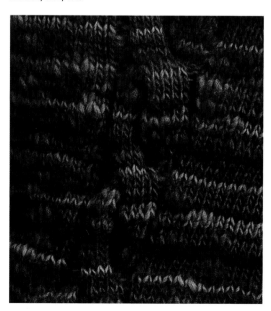

Maintaining edge sts in St st and continuing in rib, rep Inc row [every 6 rows] 13 (13, 12, 13) times, working new sts into pat—83 (89, 93, 99) sts.

Work even until sleeve measures 18½ (18½, 19, 19) inches, ending with a WS row.

Mark each end st for underarm.

Work even for 5¼ (6, 6¾, 7½) inches more, ending with a WS row.

Divide for front & back

Work 43 (45, 47, 51) sts and place on holder for front; M1, work to end of row—41 (45, 47, 49) back sts.

RIGHT BACK

Working on back sts only, work even in established pat until back yoke measures 9 (10, 11, 12) inches from underarm marker.

Bind off in pat.

RIGHT FRONT

Slip sts from holder to needle and join yarn with WS facing.

Row 1 (WS): Work even.
Row 2 (RS): Work in established rib to last 2 sts, k2tog.
Row 3: P2tog, work in established rib to end of row.
  Rep [Rows 2 and 3] 10 (10, 11, 11) times more—21 (22, 22, 24) sts.
Size extra-large only: Work 2 rows even. Bind off in pat.

LEFT SLEEVE & YOKE

Work as for right sleeve and yoke until piece measures 5¼ (6, 6¾, 7½) inches from underarm marker, ending with a WS row.

Divide for front & back
Next row (RS): Work 40 (44, 46, 48) sts, M1; place rem 43 (45, 47, 51) sts on holder for front—41 (45, 47, 49) sts.

LEFT BACK

Working on back sts only, work even in established pat until back yoke measures 9 (10, 11, 12) inches from underarm marker.
  Bind off in pat.

LEFT FRONT

Slip sts from holder to needle.
Row 1 (RS): Join yarn with RS facing; work to end of row.
Row 2: Work even.

Row 3: Ssk, work in established rib to end of row.
Row 4: Work in established pat to last 2 sts, ssp.
  Rep [Rows 3 and 4] 10 (10, 11, 11) times more—21 (22, 22, 24) sts.
Size extra-large only: Work 2 rows even. Bind off in pat.

BODY

Sew yokes tog at center back and center front along straight edge only.
  Sew sleeve seam from underarm marker to cast-on edge.
  Remove underarm markers.
  With RS facing, beg at left sleeve seam, pick up and knit across back yoke as follows: *30 (35, 39, 43) sts, pm, 16 sts, pm, 30 (35, 39, 43) sts; rep from * across front yoke, pm for beg of rnd—152 (172, 188, 204) sts.
  Working 16 sts at center front and back in Cable Panel, and rem sts in St st, work even until body measures 14½ (14½, 15, 15 ½) inches from picked-up sts.
Next 3 rnds: *K1, p1; rep from * around.
  Bind off loosely in rib.

FINISHING

Weave in ends. Block to finished measurements. ●

PROVENCE PULLOVER **SCHEMATICS**

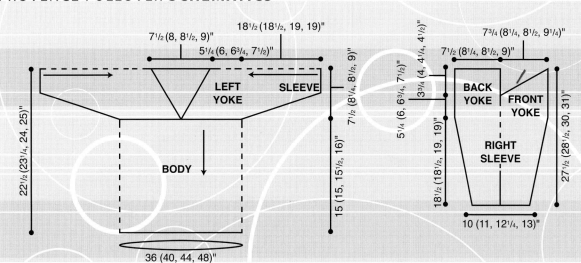

18½ (18½, 19, 19)"
7½ (8, 8½, 9)"
5¼ (6, 6¾, 7½)"
LEFT YOKE
SLEEVE
BODY
22½ (23¼, 24, 25)"
36 (40, 44, 48)"

7½ (8¼, 8½, 9)"
15 (15, 15½, 16)"
5¼ (6, 6¾, 7½)"
3¾ (4, 4¼, 4½)"
18½ (18½, 19, 19)"
7¾ (8¼, 8½, 9¼)"
7½ (8¼, 8½, 9)"
BACK YOKE
FRONT YOKE
RIGHT SLEEVE
27½ (28½, 30, 31)"
10 (11, 12¼, 13)"

STANDARD**abbreviations**

[ ] work instructions within brackets as many times as directed
( ) work instructions within parentheses in the place directed
** repeat instructions between the asterisks as directed
* repeat instructions following the single asterisk as directed
" inch(es)
approx approximately
beg begin/beginning
CC contrasting color
ch chain stitch
cm centimeter(s)
cn cable needle
dec decrease/decreases/decreasing
dpn(s) double-point needle(s)
g gram
hdc: half double crochet
inc increase/increases/increasing
k knit
k2tog knit 2 stitches together
LH left hand
m meter(s)
M1 make one stitch
MC main color
mm millimeter(s)
oz ounce(s)
p purl
pat(s) pattern(s)
p2tog purl 2 stitches together
psso pass slipped stitch over

rem remain/remaining
rep repeat(s)
rev St st reverse stockinette stitch
RH right hand
rnd(s) rounds
RS right side
sc single crochet
skp slip, knit, pass stitch over—one stitch decreased
sk2p slip 1, knit 2 together, pass slip stitch over the knit 2 together—2 stitches have been decreased
sl slip
sl 1k slip 1 knitwise
sl 1p slip 1 purlwise
sl st slip stitch(es)
ssk Slip 2 sts 1 at a time knitwise, then knit them together—a left-leaning decrease.
ssp Slip 2 sts 1 at a time knitwise, then purl them together through the back loops—a left-leaning decrease
st(s) stitch(es)
St st stockinette stitch/stocking stitch
tbl through back loop(s)
tog together
WS wrong side
wyib with yarn in back
wyif with yarn in front
yd(s) yard(s)
yfwd yarn forward
yo yarn over

SKILL**levels**

BEGINNER

Projects for first-time knitters using basic knit and purl stitches. Minimal shaping.

EASY

Projects using basic stitches, repetitive stitch patterns, simple color changes and simple shaping and finishing.

INTERMEDIATE

Projects with a variety of stitches, such as basic cables and lace, simple intarsia, double-point needles and knitting-in-the-round needle techniques, mid-level shaping and finishing.

EXPERIENCED

Projects using advanced techniques and stitches, such as short rows, Fair Isle, more intricate intarsia, cables, lace patterns and numerous color changes.

METRIC**conversion**CHART

INCHES INTO MILLIMETRES & CENTIMETRES (Rounded off slightly)

inches	mm	cm	inches	cm	inches	cm	inches	cm
1/8	3	0.3	5	12.5	21	53.5	38	96.5
1/4	6	0.6	5 1/2	14	22	56	39	99
3/8	10	1	6	15	23	58.5	40	101.5
1/2	13	1.3	7	18	24	61	41	104
5/8	15	1.5	8	20.5	25	63.5	42	106.5
3/4	20	2	9	23	26	66	43	109
7/8	22	2.2	10	25.5	27	68.5	44	112
1	25	2.5	11	28	28	71	45	114.5
1 1/4	32	3.2	12	30.5	29	73.5	46	117
1 1/2	38	3.8	13	33	30	76	47	119.5
1 3/4	45	4.5	14	35.5	31	79	48	122
2	50	5	15	38	32	81.5	49	124.5
2 1/2	65	6.5	16	40.5	33	84	50	127
3	75	7.5	17	43	34	86.5		
3 1/2	90	9	18	46	35	89		
4	100	10	19	48.5	36	91.5		
4 1/2	115	11.5	20	51	37	94		

KNITTING NEEDLES CONVERSION CHART

Canada/U.S.	0	1	2	3	4	5	6	7	8	9	10	10½	11	13	15
Metric (mm)	2	2¼	2¾	3¼	3½	3¾	4	4½	5	5½	6	6½	8	9	10

STANDARD**yarn**WEIGHT**system**

Categories of yarn, gauge ranges, and recommended needle sizes

Yarn Weight Symbol & Category Names	1 SUPER FINE	2 FINE	3 LIGHT	4 MEDIUM	5 BULKY	6 SUPER BULKY
Type of Yarns in Category	Sock, Fingering, Baby	Sport, Baby	DK, Light Worsted	Worsted, Afghan, Aran	Chunky, Craft, Rug	Bulky, Roving
Knit Gauge* Ranges in Stockinette Stitch to 4 inches	21–32 sts	23–26 sts	21–24 sts	16–20 sts	12–15 sts	6–11 sts
Recommended Needle in Metric Size Range	2.25–3.25mm	3.25–3.75mm	3.75–4.5mm	4.5–5.5mm	5.5–8mm	8mm
Recommended Needle U.S. Size Range	1 to 3	3 to 5	5 to 7	7 to 9	9 to 11	11 and larger

* GUIDELINES ONLY: The above reflect the most commonly used gauges and needle sizes for specific yarn categories.

GENERAL**information**

BASIC STITCHES
Garter Stitch
When working back and forth, knit every row. When working in the round on circular or double-point needles, knit one round then purl one round.

Stockinette Stitch
When working back and forth, knit right-side rows and purl wrong-side rows. When working in the round on circular or double-point needles, knit all rounds.

Reverse Stockinette Stitch
When working back and forth, purl right-side rows and knit wrong-side rows. When working in the round on circular or double-point needles, purl all rounds.

Ribbing
Ribbing combines knit and purl stitches within a row to give stretch to the garment. Ribbing is most often used for cuffs of hats or socks, but may be used for the entire piece.

The rib pattern is established on the first row. On subsequent rows, the knit stitches are knitted and purl stitches are purled to form the ribs.

READING PATTERN INSTRUCTIONS
Before beginning a pattern, read through it to make sure you are familiar with the abbreviations that are used.

Some patterns may be written for more than one size. In this case the smallest size is given first, and others are placed in parentheses. When only one number is given, it applies to all sizes.

You may wish to highlight the numbers for the size you are making before beginning. It is also helpful to place a self-adhesive sheet on the pattern to note any changes made while working the pattern.

MEASURING
To measure pieces, lay them flat on a smooth surface. Take the measurement in the middle of the piece, not along the outer edge where the edges tend to curve or roll.

GAUGE
The single most important factor in determining the finished size of a knit item is the gauge. Although not as important for flat, one-piece items, it is critical when making a clothing item that needs to fit properly.

It is important to make a stitch gauge swatch of at least 4 inches square with the recommended stitch patterns and needles before beginning.

Block the swatch, then measure it. If the number of stitches and rows in 4 inches are fewer than indicated under "Gauge" in the pattern, your needles are too large. Try another swatch with smaller-size needles. If the number of stitches and rows are more than indicated under "Gauge" in the pattern, your needles are too small. Try another swatch with larger-size needles.

Continue to adjust needles until correct gauge is achieved.

WORKING FROM CHARTS
Charts are provided both for more complicated stitch patterns as well as color work. On the chart each square represents one stitch. A key is given indicating the color or stitch represented by each color or symbol in the box.

The row number is always given at the side of the chart where the row begins. If the number is at the right (usually right-side, odd-numbered rows), read right to left; if it is at the left (usually wrong-side, even-numbered rows), read left to right.

For color-work charts, rows beginning at the right represent the right side of the work and are usually knit. Rows beginning at the left represent the wrong side and are usually purled.

When working in rounds, every row on the chart is a right-side row, and is read from right to left.

USE OF ZERO
In patterns that include various sizes, zeros are sometimes necessary. For example, k0 (0, 1) means if you are making the smallest or middle size, you would do nothing, and if you are making the largest size, you would k1.

GLOSSARY

bind off—used to finish an edge

cast on—process of making foundation stitches used in knitting

decrease—means of reducing the number of stitches in a row

increase—means of adding to the number of stitches in a row

intarsia—method of knitting a multicolored pattern into the fabric

knitwise—insert needle into stitch as if to knit

make 1—method of increasing using the strand between the last stitch worked and the next stitch

place marker—placing a purchased marker or loop of contrasting yarn onto the needle for ease in working a pattern repeat

purlwise—insert needle into stitch as if to purl

right side—side of garment or piece that will be seen when worn

selvage (selvedge) stitch—edge stitch used to make seaming easier

slip, slip, knit—Method of making a left-leaning decrease by moving stitches from left needle to right needle and working them together.

slip stitch—an unworked stitch slipped from left needle to right needle, usually as if to purl

wrong side—side that will be inside when garment is worn

work even—continue to work in the pattern as established without working any increases or decreases

work in pattern as established—continue to work following the pattern stitch as it has been set up or established on the needle, working any increases or decreases in such a way that the established pattern remains the same

yarn over—method of increasing by wrapping the yarn over the right needle without working a stitch

KNITTING**basics**

KNIT (K)

With yarn in back, insert tip of right needle from front to back in next stitch on left needle.

Bring yarn counterclockwise around the tip of the right needle.

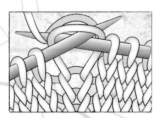

Pull yarn loop through the stitch with right needle point.

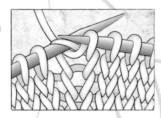

Slide the stitch off the left needle. The new stitch is on the right needle.

PURL (P)

With yarn in front, insert tip of right needle from back to front through front loop of the next stitch on the left needle.

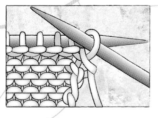

Bring yarn around the right needle counterclockwise.

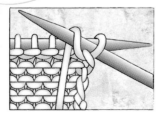

With right needle, draw yarn back through the stitch.

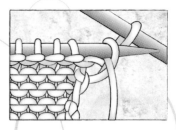

Slide the stitch off the left needle. The new stitch is on the right needle.

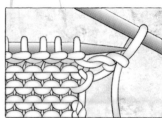

INCREASE (INC)
Two stitches in one stitch
Increase (knit)

Knit the next stitch in the usual manner, but don't remove the stitch from the left needle.

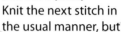

Place right needle behind left needle and knit again into the back of the same stitch. Slip original stitch off left needle.

Increase (purl)

Purl the next stitch in the usual manner, but don't remove the stitch from the left needle.

Place right needle behind left needle and purl again into the back of the same stitch. Slip original stitch off left needle.

MAKE 1 INCREASE (M1)
Invisible Increase

Insert left needle from front to back under the horizontal loop between the last stitch worked and next stitch on left needle.

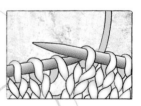

With right needle, knit into the back of this loop.

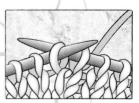

Backward Loop Increase over the right needle

With your thumb, make a loop over the right needle.

Slip the loop from your thumb onto the needle and pull to tighten.

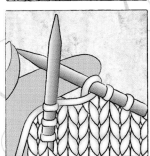

Increase in top of stitch below

Insert tip of right needle into the stitch on left needle one row below.

Knit this stitch, then knit the stitch on the left needle.

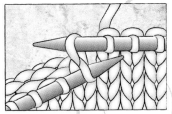

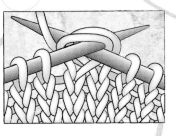

DECREASE (DEC)
Knit 2 together (k2tog)

Put tip of right needle through next two stitches on left needle as to knit. Knit these two stitches as one.

Purl 2 together (p2tog)

Put tip of right needle through next two stitches on left needle as to purl. Purl these two stitches as one.

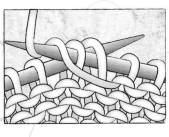

Slip, Slip, Knit (ssk)

Slip next two stitches, one at a time, as if to knit from left needle to right needle.

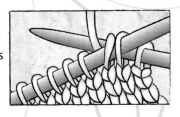

Insert left needle in front of both stitches and knit them together as one.

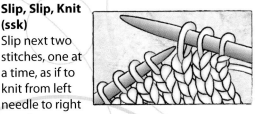

Slip, Slip, Purl (ssp)

Slip next two stitches, one at a time, as if to knit from left needle to right needle. Slip these stitches back onto left needle keeping them twisted.

Purl these two stitches together through back loops.

CROCHET**basics**

Some knit items are finished with a crochet trim or edging. Below are some abbreviations used in crochet and a review of some basic crochet stitches.

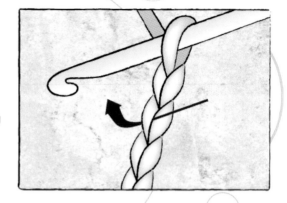

CHAIN STITCH (CH)

Begin by making a slip knot on the hook. Bring the yarn over the hook from back to front and draw through the loop on the hook.

For each additional chain stitch, bring the yarn over the hook from back to front and draw through the loop on the hook.

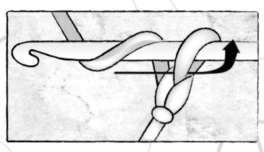

HALF DOUBLE CROCHET (HDC)

Yo, insert hook in st, yo, pull through st, yo, pull through all 3 lps on hook.

SINGLE CROCHET (SC)

Insert the hook in the second chain through the center of the V. Bring the yarn over the hook from back to front.
Draw the yarn through the chain stitch and onto the hook.

Again bring yarn over the hook from back to front and draw it through both loops on hook.

For additional rows of single crochet, insert the hook under both loops of the previous stitch instead of through the center of the V as when working into the chain stitch.

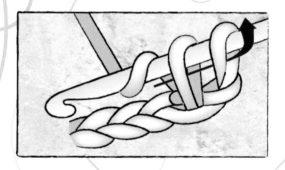

SLIP STITCH (SL ST)

Insert hook under both loops of the stitch, bring yarn over the hook from back to front and draw it through the stitch and the loop on the hook.

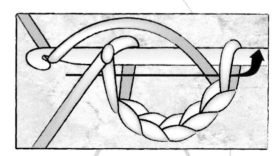

WORKING**in**THE**round**

Working With Double-Point Needles
Helpful Tips:
Make sure that the cast on edge remains along the inside of the circle on each needle. This will help prevent the stitches from twisting around the needles.

Slip the first cast-on stitch from the left-hand needle tip to the right-hand needle tip. Slip the last cast-on stitch from the right-hand needle tip up and over the stitch just transferred and onto the left-hand needle tip to "join" into a ring.

4 Double-Point Needles
Cast on the number of stitches required. Distribute the stitches as instructed in the pattern on 3 double-point needles. Position the needles so that needle 1 is on the left and needle 3 is on the right. The yarn you're about to work with should be attached to the last stitch on needle 3.

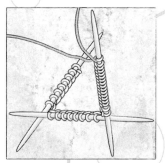

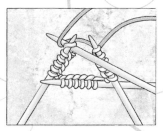

5 Double-Point Needles
Cast on the number of stitches required. Distribute stitches evenly on 4 double-point needles. Position the needles so that needle 1 is on the left and needle 4 is on the right. The yarn you're about to work with should be attached to the last stitch on needle 4.

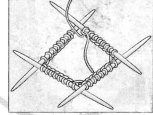

KITCHENER**stitch**

This method of grafting with two needles is used for the toes of socks and flat seams. To graft the edges together and form an unbroken line of stockinette stitch, divide all stitches evenly onto two knitting needles—one behind the other. Thread yarn into tapestry needle. Hold needles with wrong sides of fabric together and work from right to left as follows:

Step 1: Insert tapestry needle into first stitch on front needle as if to purl. Draw yarn through stitch, leaving stitch on knitting needle.

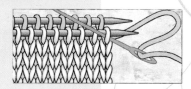

Step 2: Insert tapestry needle into the first stitch on the back needle as if to purl. Draw yarn through stitch and slip stitch off knitting needle.

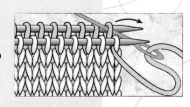

Step 3: Insert tapestry needle into the next stitch on same (back) needle as if to knit, leaving stitch on knitting needle.

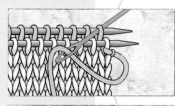

Step 4: Insert tapestry needle into the first stitch on the front needle as if to knit. Draw yarn through stitch and slip stitch off knitting needle.

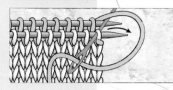

Step 5: Insert tapestry needle into the next stitch on same (front) needle as if to purl. Draw yarn through stitch, leaving stitch on knitting needle.

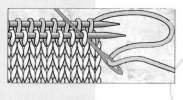

Repeat Steps 2 through 5 until one stitch is left on each needle. Then, repeat Steps 2 and 4. Fasten off. Grafted stitches should be the same size as the adjacent knitted stitches.

INTARSIA

In certain patterns there are larger areas of color within the piece. Since this type of pattern requires a new color only for that section, it is not necessary to carry the yarn back and forth across the back. For this type of color change, a separate ball of yarn or bobbin is used for each color, making the yarn available only where needed. Bring the new yarn being used up-and-around the yarn just worked; this will "lock" the colors and prevent holes from occurring at the join.

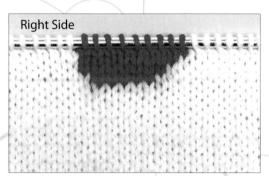
Right Side

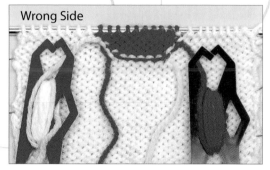
Wrong Side

SEAM**finishes**

MATTRESS SEAM

This type of seam can be used for vertical seams (like side seams). It is worked with the right sides of the pieces facing you, making it easier to match stitches for stripe patterns. It is worked between the first and second stitch at the edge of the piece and works best when the first stitch is a selvage stitch.

To work this seam, thread a tapestry needle with matching yarn. Insert the needle into one corner of work from back to front, just above the cast on stitch, leaving a 3-inch tail. Take needle to edge of other piece and bring it from back to front at the corner of this piece.

Return to the first piece and insert the needle from the right to wrong side where the thread comes out of the piece. Slip the needle upward under one horizontal thread and bring the needle through to the right side.

Cross to the other side and repeat the same process "down where you came out, under one thread and up."

Continue working back and forth on the two pieces in the same manner for about an inch, then gently pull on the thread pulling the two pieces together. (Photo A)

Complete the seam and fasten off. Use the beginning tail to even-up the lower edge by working a figure 8 between the cast-on stitches at the corners. Insert the threaded needle from front to back under both threads of the corner cast-on stitch on the edge opposite the tail, then into the same stitch on the first edge. Pull gently until the figure 8 fills the gap. (Photo B)

Photo A

Photo B

When a project is made with a textured yarn that will not pull easily through the pieces, it is recommended that a smooth yarn of the same color be used to work the seam.

GARTER STITCH SEAMS

The "bumps" of the garter stitch selvage nestle between each other in a garter stitch seam, often producing a nearly reversible seam. This is a good seam for afghan strips and blocks of the same color. Starting as for the mattress seam, work from bump to bump, alternating sides. In this case you enter each stitch only once.

3-NEEDLE BIND-OFF

Use this technique for seaming two edges together, such as when joining a seam. Hold the live edge stitches on two separate needles with right sides of the fabric together.

With a third needle, knit together a stitch from the front needle with one from the back.

Repeat, knitting a stitch from the front needle with one from the back needle once more.

Slip the first stitch over the second.

Repeat knitting, a front and back pair of stitches together, then bind one pair off.

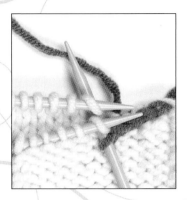

MATCHING**patterns**

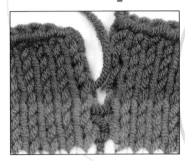

When it comes to matching stripes and other elements in a design, a simple formula makes things line up perfectly:

Begin the seam in the usual way.

Enter the first stitch of each new color stripe (or pattern detail) on the same side as you began the seam; i.e. the same side as your tail.

KNITTING**with**BEADS

Threading beads onto yarn is the most common way to knit with beads.

Step 1: Before beginning to knit, thread the beads onto your skein of yarn using a bead threader. As you work, unwind a small quantity of yarn, each time sliding the beads towards the ball until needed. Pass the yarn through the loop of the threader and pick up beads with the working end of the needle.

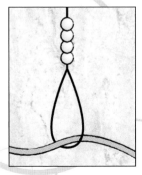

Step 2: Slide the beads over the loop and onto the yarn.

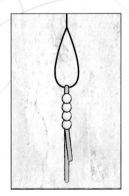

FELTINGinstructions

THE FELT FORMULA

Felting is not a precise science. Wool felts when exposed to water, heat and agitation, but each element is hard to control precisely. As a result, each individual project may vary in the way it felts.

Felting can be done in the sink, but washing machines get the job done more quickly. Each washing machine is different, and the rate at which specific machines felt a piece will vary. So, be sure to follow the specific felting instructions of the piece you are making, and check your piece several times during the felting process to make sure you are getting the desired results.

The felting process releases fibers which can clog your washing machine. Therefore, you may want to place items in a zippered pillowcase before putting them in the washing machine. Also, adding other laundry, such as jeans, when felting will increase the amount of agitation and speed up the process. Be careful not to use items that shed fibers of their own, such as towels.

FELTING FACTS

Felting a knit or crochet piece makes it shrink. Therefore, the piece you knit must start out much larger than the finished felted size will be. Shrinkage varies because there are so many factors that affect it. These variables include water temperature, the hardness of the water, how much (and how long) the piece is agitated, the amount and type of soap used, yarn brand, fiber content and color.

You can control how much your piece felts by watching it closely. Check your piece after about 10 minutes to see how quickly it is felting. Look at the stitch definition and size to determine if the piece has been felted enough.

HOW TO FELT

Place items to be felted in the washing machine along with one tablespoon of dish detergent and a pair of jeans or other laundry. (Remember, do not felt projects with other clothing that release their own fibers.) Set washing machine on smallest load and use hot water. Start machine and check progress after ten minutes. Check progress more frequently after piece starts to felt. Reset the machine if needed to continue the agitation cycle. Do not allow machine to go to spin cycle; rapid spinning can cause creases in the felted fabric that may be very difficult to get out later. As the piece becomes more felted, you may need to pull it into shape.

When the piece has felted to the desired size, rinse it by hand in warm water. Remove the excess water by rolling in a towel and squeezing.

Block the piece into shape, and let air dry. Do not dry in clothes dryer. For pieces that need to conform to a particular shape (such as a hat or purse), stuff the piece with a towel to help it hold its shape while drying. Felted items are very strong, so don't be afraid to push and pull it into the desired shape. It may take several hours or several days for the pieces to dry completely.

After the piece is completely dry, excess fuzziness can be trimmed with scissors if a smoother surface is desired, or the piece can be brushed for a fuzzier appearance.

YARN**resources**

Many of the yarns presented in this book are available in your local yarn shop. If you should have any problems purchasing them in your area, the list below will serve as a helpful resource.

Artyarns
(914) 428-0333
www.artyarns.com

Berroco Inc.
(508) 278-2527
www.berroco.com

Blue Sky Alpacas
(888) 460-8862
www.blueskyalpacas.com

Brown Sheep Co. Inc.
(800) 826-9136
www.brownsheep.com

Classic Elite Yarns
(978) 453-2837
www.classiceliteyarns.com

Crystal Palace Yarns
www.straw.com

DMC Corp.
(973) 589-0606
www.dmc-usa.com

The Fibre Company
(215) 687-5534
www.thefibreco.com

Knit One Crochet Too Inc.
(207) 892-9625
www.knitonecrochettoo.com

Knit Picks
(800) 574-1323
www.knitpicks.com

Knitting Fever Inc. (Elsebeth Lavold)
(516) 546-3600
www.knittingfever.com

Misti Alpaca Inc.
(888) 776-9276
www.mistialpaca.com

Mirasol
www.mirasolperu.com

Nashua Handknits
(800) 445-9276
www.nashuaknits.com

Patons
(888) 368-8401
www.patonsyarns.com

Plymouth Yarn Co. Inc.
(215) 788-0459
www.plymouthyarn.com

Rowan (RYC)
(800) 445-9276
www.knitrowan.com

Schaefer Yarn Co.
(607) 532-9452
www.schaeferyarn.com

ShiBuiKnits
(503) 595-5898
www.shibuiknits.com

SR Kertzer
(800) 263-2354
www.kertzer.com

**Tahki/Stacy Charles Inc.
(Tahki, Filatura Di Crosa)**
(800) 338-YARN (9276)
www.tahkistacycharles.com

Unique Kolours (Colinette)
(800) 25-2dye4 (252-3934)
www.uniquekolours.com

SUGGESTED READING

Knitting Without Tears by Elizabeth Zimmermann, *Knitting from the Top Down* by Barbara Walker, *Seamless Sweaters* by Sidna Farley, *The Twisted Sisters Knit Sweaters: A Knit-to-Fit Workshop* by Lynne Vogel, *Knitting Cuff to Cuff (12 Sweaters One Way)* by Susan Guagliumi

PHOTO**index**

TAKEit FROMthe TOP-down

Aztec Top, 92

Structured Rib Pullover, 96

Gone Downtown Top, 101

Mock Mobius Cowl, 104

Shell Tote, 106

Listado Lace Cowl, 108

Slip Stitch Sack, 110

Daisy's Dress & Cap, 112

Bell-Bottom Bambini, 116

Tulip Lace Tunic and Hat, 120

Totally Seamless Jumper, 125

STEPPINGitUP aNOTCH: knitting INnew DIRECTIONS

Sophie's Shrug, 130

Lizzie Cropped Cardi, 134

Kid's Cuff-to-Cuff Top, 137

Little Bit o' Sugar, 140

Chain-Link Cardigan, 143

Casual Side-to-Side Vest, 147

Celtic Vine Hat & Fingerless Gloves, 150

Just the Right Jacket, 154

Provence Pullover, 158

SPECIAL**thanks**

This book would not be a success without the talents of the following designers. We would like to thank them for contributing their imaginative designs to help make this book possible.

Jean Clement
Woodland Rose Tunic, 54
Shazzam Pullover, 68
Aztec Top, 92

Ellen Edwards Drechsler
Little Bit o' Sugar, 140

Lorraine Ehrlinger
Sweetie Pie Stripes, 30

Lisa Ellis
Restauranteur Shawl, 22
Slip Stitch Sack, 110

Faina Goberstein
Structured Rib Pullover, 96

Kara Gott Warner
Café au Lait Cardigan, 15

Ava Lynne Green
Mom & Me Felted Booties, 72

Sara Louise Harper
Easy One-Piece Cardigan, 8
Enchanted Forest, 42

Katharine Hunt
Mystical Mosaic Vest, 18
Hunky Man Jacket, 25

Andra Knight-Bowman
All About Entrelac, 34
Simple Summer Sweater, 80
Casual Side-to-Side Vest, 147

Shirley MacNulty
Salamanca Skirt, 61

Amy Marshall
Fleur Jumper, 83

Simona Merchant-Dest
Gone Downtown Top, 101
Daisy's Dress & Cap, 112
Tulip Lace Tunic and Hat, 120

Laura Nelkin
Listado Lace Cowl, 108
Bell-Bottom Bambini, 116
Sophie's Shrug, 130

Amy Polcyn
Tribeca Belted Cardigan, 38
Chain-Link Cardigan, 143

Pauline Schultz
Totally Seamless Jumper, 125
Just the Right Jacket, 154

Ann Squire
Clementine Felted Carryall, 87
Mock Mobius Cowl, 104

Ann Weaver
Bohemian Rhapsody, 46
Jacob's Ladder, 64

KyleAnn Williams
Everyone Loves Chocolate, 12
Kid's Cuff-to-Cuff Top, 137

Sarah Wilson
Mellifera, 76

Lois S. Young
Shell Tote, 106

Diane Zangl
Lizzie Cropped Cardi, 134
Celtic Vine Hat & Fingerless Gloves, 150
Provence Pullover, 158